BAG BOOK

Over **500** Great Uses
—and reuses—
for Paper, Plastic and other Bags
to Organize & Enhance Your Life

by

Vicki Lansky

illustrations by
Martha Campbell

book trade distribution
Publishers Group West

BOOK PEDDLERS
Minnetonka, MN

Special thanks go to
Susan Bramson, Kathryn Ring and Abby Herstein,
Ziploc® Brand and Slide-Loc® Bags by S.C. Johnson.

ISBN 0-916773-89-2

copyright© 2000 by Vicki Lansky
first printing September 2000

Publisher's Cataloging-in-Publication
(Provided by Quality Books, Inc.)

Lansky, Vicki.
    The bag book : over 500 great uses and reuses
for paper, plastic, and other bags to organize &
enhance your life/by Vicki Lansky ;
illustrations by Martha Campbell.
    p.cm.
    Includes index.
    ISBN: 0-916773-89-2

    1. Bags. 2. Home economics. I. Title.

TS198.B3L362000   688.8
                          QB199-500577

BOOK PEDDLERS
15245 Minnetonka Blvd, Minnetonka, MN 55345
952 /912-0036 • fax: 952/912-0105
www.bookpeddlers.com

printed in the USA

00   01   02   03   04   05   06   5   4   3   2   1

TABLE OF CONTENTS

introduction

introduction

Some folks might think that the wheel was the significant invention of civilization. Personally, I'm leaning toward THE BAG! Bags, be they paper, plastic or something else, are probably the most valuable commodities of our society. *(How would we get our groceries home? Take our garbage out? Shop?)*

We do take these simple 'holding devices' for granted but maybe we shouldn't. Bags touch every aspect of our lives. And it's these other uses—both the obvious and the not-so-obvious—that make the bag, in all its various configurations, such an important part of our lives.

The word "bag" has become such a large part of our vocabulary that we don't even realize just how pervasive it is. Study this list for a moment and you'll understand what I mean.

Air bag
Airsickness bag
Baby bag
Bag of bones
Bag of wind
Bag lady *(homeless woman with all her possessions in a shopping bag)*
Barf bag *(disposable bag provided by airlines for motion sickness)*
Beach bag
Bean bag
Boil-in-a-bag
Book bag
Bowling bag
Boston bag *(a two-handled bag for carrying books, papers, etc.)*
Brown bag *(a lunch term)*
Caddie bag
Camera bag
Canvas bag
Carpet bag
Carry-on bag
Clutch bag
Cosmetic bag
Ditty bag
Doggy bag
Douglas bag *(airtight bag used to collect expired air)*

Duffel bag
Evening bag
Feed bag
Flight bag
Freezer bag
Garment bag
Gift bag
Gladstone bag *(light, hand luggage composed of two hinged compartments)*
Golf bag
Goodie bag
Grab bag
Grocery bag
Gunny-bag
Handbag
Hot-water bag
Ice bag
In the bag
Kit bag *(as in knapsack for a soldier)*
Lunch bag
Mail bag
Mesh bag
Mixed bag
Musk bag *(the musk-secreting gland of a musk deer)*
Mummy bag
Old bag
Overnight bag
Post-bag *(for mail)*
Punching bag
Roll bag *(a small, zippered duffel for carrying school supplies)*
Saddle bag
Sand bag
Sandwich bag
Sea bag
Shopping bag
Shoulder bag
Sleeping bag
Storage bag
String bag
Stuff bag
Tea bag
Tote bag
Toy bag
Trash bag
Tucker bag *(a bag used to carry food in Australia)*
Vacuum bag
Weekend bag
Wind bag
Wine bag

But it's those "not-so-obvious" uses that have intrigued me. As a helpful hints contributing editor for *Family Circle* Magazine for over 10 years, I've been collecting "another use for" ideas for a whole variety of household items. I found over 500 uses for baking soda and over 350 uses for transparent tape *(and I have a book on each to prove it)* so it was not so far-fetched when I realized there were enough "other" great uses for bags that a lot of us would enjoy learning about—uses that also help us organize our lives.

I would not be at all embarassed to be known as the "Bag Lady" *(though my children will probably be)* if this becomes a best-selling collection of uses for bags! My new definition for "Bag Lady" is *'one-who-has-written-the-book-on-bags.'*

No, I do not sit around and think up and test each of these ideas. (I *do* have a life.) I've learned about and heard about these uses from you, the "bag-ger." I'm a collector of tips. For me, the fun is that I get to share these great ideas with everyone.

—*Vicki Lansky*

Chapter One

THE BAG
A Bit of History

Obviously, mankind has used flexible containers (i.e., bags) from earliest times. After all, our prehistoric ancestors were nomads and, when you move around all the time, you've got to have something in which to carry your "stuff." Those folks needed pouches for holding arrows and the like, too. The first bags were probably made from animal skins and dried organs such as bladders or stomachs. Grass materials—woven—were also the stuff that containers were made of. When people learned to weave fiber, they could then use fabric for making various pouches and packs. The transition from fiber bags to paper bags is hard to pinpoint historically. Paper has a long and varied history starting with the basic papyrus back in the days of early Egypt.

Today we have dramatically increased the variety of uses for bags because we make them not only from paper and fabric but also from plastic, making them much more versatile. The manufacturing processes of the Industrial Revolution created a whole new genre of bags because of the need for convenience. Our Industrial Revolution also produced the concept of waste and therefore the need for waste containers.

Paper Bags

The familiar paper grocery bag, the one with the flat bottom and collapsible sides, is a little more than 100 years old. Charles Stilwell—a Union soldier turned inventor—is credited with the invention. He produced the first machine-made folding paper bag—a vast improvement on the V-shaped, hand-pasted bags then available. Stilwell dubbed his new bag the S.O.S. for "Self-Opening Sack." Stilwell's sack folded flat for easy storage, but with one hand it could be snapped open and would stand on its own. But Stilwell's invention really did not take off until the 1930s, when the supermarket concept developed and expanded. This tied in with large home refrigerators, freezers and the use of cars. People now shopped in quantity for the whole week rather than just purchasing one day's food. Stilwell's S.O.S., which could be easily stored, quickly opened and efficiently filled with groceries, soon became a staple to the industry. But it also became indispensable to shoppers, who found a variety of uses for it in their homes for such varied things as trash and Halloween masks.

Before the advent of cash register tapes and printed receipts (which was also before bar codes and scanning), the paper bag was also the paper on which the prices were jotted down and added up, giving the paper bag a second purpose. The low cost of paper and the advent of giant-economy-size, prepackaged products worked hand in hand with the need for cheap—and disposable—containers to carry home bulky items. Today, of course, paper bags tell where you shopped and even have become a medium of advertising unto themselves. Paper grocery bags are so much a part of our world today that even the dictionary defines the word "bag" as "a usually flexible container <a grocery bag >."

Plastic Bags

Do you remember a time before plastic bags? I do. (*And, if you're of a certain age, too, then you must remember the bowls in the fridge that were covered with waxed paper and a rubber band, or a very primitive form of plastic bowl cover with stretched out elastic that looked like a shower cap.*) Or, maybe your family used glass refrigerator dishes with lids that never really fit tight, butcher paper, waxed sandwich bags or any of the other methods housekeepers improvised to store food B.P.E. (*Before the Plastic Era*). Now we have plastic bags galore in every size, shape and closure imaginable.

The plastic bag industry (yes, there is an actual Plastic Bag Association) has documented the history of the introduction of plastic bag usage in our economy. Here is their time line, combined with others we have found:

1957-   The first bags and sandwich bags on a roll were introduced.

1958-   Poly dry cleaning bags began to compete with traditional brown paper.

1965-   Mobil Corp. launched the plastic Baggie (and later added a tuck-in flap).

1966-   Plastic bag use in bread packaging took over 25% to 30% of the market.

1966-   Plastic produce bags on a roll were introduced in grocery stores.

1969-   The New York City Sanitation Department's "New York City Experiment" demonstrated that plastic refuse bag curbside pickup was cleaner, safer and quieter than metal trash can pickup, beginning a shift to plastic can liners among consumers.

1970-   Dow Chemical unveiled the Ziploc® brand
          Bag—the original "pinch-n-seal" bag.

1973-   The first commercial system for manufacturing
          plastic grocery bags became operational.

1974/75- Retailing giants such as Sears, JC Penney,
          Montgomery Ward, Jordan Marsh, Allied, Feder-
          ated and Hills made the switch to plastic merchan-
          dise bags.

1977-   The handled plastic grocery bag (aka the "T-shirt"
          bag) was introduced to the supermarket indus-
          try as an alternative to paper sacks.

1981-   The "T-shirt" bag became a major force in the bag
          market. First year significant tonnage production
          was recorded.

1982-   Kroger and Safeway started to replace traditional
          kraft sacks with polyethylene "T-shirt" bags.

1990-   Consumer plastic bag recycling began through
          supermarket collection site network.

1990s-   The OneZip *(snaps over dual plastic tracks and
          slides like a gondola on a cable)* bag was developed
          during the early 1990s by Mobil Corp.

1992-   Nearly half of U.S. supermarkets had recycling
          available for plastic bags.

1996-   Four of five grocery bags used were plastic.

The Paper-or-Plastic Dilemma

Today we are confronted, at the supermarket, with the question at the check-out—"Do you want paper or plastic bags?" The environmental concerns play both ways, making it difficult to know which is really the better choice. You can simplify the decision by following these rules:
- Whatever you choose, reuse.
- Use it up or wear it out.

The shopping bags—any bags you get—require natural resources and energy to manufacture and transport. When you bring the bags back to reuse, you conserve resources and reduce waste. Some grocery stores will give you a five-cent or ten-cent credit for every bag you reuse.

It is certainly a reasonable idea to include reuse and waste reduction in your shopping routine. Keep clean bags in a convenient spot, such as with your shopping list or in your car. Wash and reuse plastic produce bags. If you don't need a bag, say so.

Most Americans don't seem to be willing to get into the habit of bringing their own canvas or string bags with them to the grocery store the way people do in other countries. (*We aren't called the "Throw-Away Society" for nothing.*) Although we might worry about whether or not it's the "environmentally correct" choice, most of us would not be willing to go back to a life without plastic bags—although we are concerned about how long bags take to break down in landfill sites—especially since they can be used for so many things, besides carrying groceries.

Every time you reuse a plastic bag you double the environmental savings: 1) you save the bag you reused from going to a landfill and, 2) you save a new one from needing to be used.

According to Dr. William Rathje of the University of Arizona's Garbage Project, nothing degrades fast enough to extend the useful lives of modern U.S. landfills—not paper, not plastics—nothing.

Compared to paper grocery bags, plastic grocery bags are said to:
◻ Consume 40% less energy than paper when made
◻ Generate 80% less solid waste
◻ Produce 70% fewer atmospheric emissions
◻ Release up to 94% fewer waterborne wastes

Since 1990, many grocery stores have made plastic bag recycle bins available, allowing you to bring excess bags to a site so they can be put to better use than a landfill. Today, recycled bags are processed and made into wood-polymer lumber that's used for making decks, boardwalks, nature trails and park benches, outdoor furniture, speed bumps and parking barriers.

And, while we now have many more bag varieties than we did in the "old days"—(paper and plastic come in sizes and formats too numerous to mention)—there's still a place for cloth, mesh and net bags. They're good for the environment because they can be used over and over and, in some situations, no other bag will do. It is a habit worth developing.

But since we are not about to become a paper- or plastic-"less" bag society, I hope you will find many new uses—and re-uses—for the bags you have on hand. Read on!

Chapter Two

PAPER BAGS

The ubiquitous brown paper grocery bag touches our lives every time we go to the grocery store. These bags are made from kraft paper...a word of Northern European origin that means "strength"—and strong it is, because each bag can hold up to twenty pounds of groceries. Some stores offer grocery bags with sturdy paper handles, making them even more user-friendly. Other stores "quietly" carry them, making them available only when specifically requested. (I know of some people who have "switched" stores just to have handled bags to bring their groceries home.) One of the paper bag's best features is that it can be reused, making it environmentally friendly.

The Paper Bag Council (part of the American Forest and Paper Association) is a group of eleven companies that make the paper used for paper grocery bags. They support a campaign to encourage families to reuse and recycle their paper grocery bags developed by Mark Ahlness, a third grade teacher, called the "Earth Day Grocery Project." Every April they coordinate schools and local grocery stores to give out thousands of hand-decorated brown bags to celebrate Earth Day and to increase environmental awareness (www.earthdaybags.org).

While the plastic industry has probably taken the lead in the use of bags, the paper bag is still an important staple.

In this chapter, you'll find many more home uses for that grocery bag and its "baby cousin," the brown paper lunch bag, than you probably ever thought of. The size of the job you need done will determine which size works best for you.

AROUND THE HOUSE

In the Kitchen

Probably the most common use for a brown paper bag is as the garbage bag. Whether you line your kitchen trash can with one, or just substitute a bag alone for your trash holder, it is usually the bag of choice. We do know that, as paper, it breaks down faster than plastic, so it seems to be a better environmental choice.

It's a good idea to put a piece of folded newspaper (or other liner, such as half an egg carton or a used plastic bag) at the bottom of a paper bag to absorb any dampness from waste that may make for a soggy bottom. If dampness causes you to lose a bag's contents, then using a brown bag for garbage has become an exercise in futility.

Using a single, large plastic bag to line a trash container, with brown bags inside the plastic-lined container, can be a good idea and good compromise on the paper vs. plastic issue. The plastic bag will protect the kitchen trash container for those times when the paper bag disintegrates, saving you a messy clean-up when the whole lot—plastic and paper—must be tossed out together.

Being Counter Productive

• Eliminate splattering when whipping cream by cutting an appropriately-sized opening in a brown paper bag and wrapping it around the mixer bowl, keeping the opening toward you.

• Cover countertops or sink with an opened grocery bag for messy chores such as peeling, grating and chopping vegetables. When you finish, roll up the mess in the bag and dispose of it all in one step.

• Cut up a brown paper bag and use it to drain bacon (and other fried foods) and to cool cookies.

• Put a frozen turkey in a large brown bag, if you are defrosting it on a counter, to prevent the outside of the turkey from reaching room temperature while the inside is still thawing. Raw turkey (i.e., the outside of the turkey) at room temperature is subject to spoilage.

Shake It Up

• Put French fries in a paper bag, add salt and shake. This saves on expensive paper towels and absorbs grease just as well.

• Serve popcorn in a paper bag. It's easy to salt the popcorn, then give it a few shakes while holding the bag closed, and the bag keeps the popcorn fresh.

PLEASE, not "IN THE BAG"

Even though you may have heard that it's okay to cook or reheat foods in brown paper bags, DON'T! According to a United States Department of Agriculture warning issued in May of 1998, it's not safe to cook in brown bags in an oven or a microwave. They are not sanitary, may cause a fire and can emit toxic fumes. Cook in an oven cooking bag made for this purpose.

En papillote -the French way of oven cooking "in a bag" keeps whatever is inside moist. It really cooks by steaming, so you don't have to add very much fat. It's not an ordinary bag, but oiled parchment in which meat or fish can be wrapped and baked.

Just "Ripe"

• Ripen fruits and vegetables such as peaches, avocados, pears, apples or tomatoes by storing them in a paper bag on the counter along with (or even without) a ripe apple. The paper helps retain the natural gases that ripen the fruit—the ripe apple gives off these gases. Check often and stop the ripening process when the fruit is ready by moving items to the refrigerator.

• Wrap green bananas in a damp dish towel and place them in a brown paper bag to ripen. (Again, putting them in the fridge stops the ripening.)

• Dry fresh herbs by tying them in loose bundles and hanging them upside down in paper bags in a warm, dry room or garage. When dry, remove the stalks and run a rolling pin over the bags to crush the dried herbs before putting them in an air-tight glass container.

Food Storage

• Store mushrooms in a small brown paper bag in the refrigerator to keep them fresh.

• Keep onions from sprouting for two to three months by removing them from their mesh or plastic bag and putting them in a brown paper bag on the bottom shelf of the refrigerator.

• Store ice cubes in a brown paper bag to keep them from sticking together.

Cool It

• Make a temporary cooler by washing out empty gallon or half-gallon plastic milk containers. Fill them three-quarters full of water, screw the lids on tightly and freeze. Line the bottom of a brown paper grocery bag with several layers of folded news-paper, at least an inch thick. Place the container of ice on the newspaper. Arrange cold foods and drinks in the bag. Fold over the top of the bag and staple it tightly to close.

Laundry Aids

• Tear open a dampened paper bag along the seams and use it as an emergency pressing cloth.

• Keep a wool sweater or other stretchy knit in shape by spreading it on a brown paper bag and tracing its shape before washing it. Then, after washing, arrange the washed sweater on the paper to dry and gently work it to fit the pattern.

Cleaning Clout

• Secure a large brown paper bag over the head of your dust mop and shake it. You'll keep the dirt and dust contained and easy to dispose of.

- Tape or pin a small paper bag to your apron or belt when you start cleaning and drop in those little items, such as pins, crayons and scraps of paper, that you find along the way.

- Clean silk flowers by shaking them, with some salt, in a brown paper bag.

Household 'Hold-It' Help

- Need to spray paint a small item? Place it in a large brown paper shopping bag and spray paint it inside the bag. Then just throw the bag away after the item is dry.

- Tape a small paper bag on the wall under the spot where you are going to drill a hole to catch the excess "excavation." This makes for a fast, easy clean-up.

Grease-Be-Gone

- Remove wax from tablecloths or carpets by placing an opened brown bag on the problem and quickly running a warm iron over it. Greasy spots will appear on the bag as the grease is absorbed. Move a clean paper area to the spot and continue until no more grease appears.

- Use the same method to remove grease marks from wallpaper. Apply a warm iron over an opened brown bag to absorb grease marks. Repeat, using clean parts of the bag, until all the grease is absorbed.

Paper Recycling Collection

- Store used newspapers (as well as other items that can be recycled) in large paper grocery bags. The handled bags are especially convenient for storing and then carrying recycling items out.

Something You "Auto" Know

- Save yourself the trouble of scraping snow and ice off your car's windshield by placing a torn-open paper bag beneath the windshield wipers after you've parked the car. Just peel it off when you're ready to leave.

• Tear a ten-inch strip along the back seam of a brown grocery bag. Slip the bag over your car steering wheel on a hot day and the wheel will stay cool and touchable.

• Absorb car grease before it reaches your garage floor by placing an opened brown bag on the floor under your parked car to catch drips. Change the bag when timely.

Light Your Fire
• Stuff a paper lunch bag with some crumpled newspaper and ends or bits of candle wax for a good fire starter.

Breathe Right
• Breathe into a brown paper bag if you begin to hyperventilate. It forces you to re-inhale the CO_2 which will stabilize the problem.

Postal Packing
•Use cut-open brown paper grocery bags to wrap packages for mailing. You save money on special mailing paper and recycle bags at the same time.

• Use a lunch bag as a mailing envelope. (The maximum size allowable is 6-1/8 inches by 11-1/2 inches.) The top can be folded down to meet length requirements and stapled or taped shut. Two can be taped together to do a larger job.

Festive Occasions
• Make your own luminaries. Cut small, decorative patterns on the larger sides of small brown bags with flat bottoms and fill with about two inches of sand. Once you've put them in place to outline a driveway or sidewalk, place a small, lighted votive

candle in the center of the sand, at the bottom of each bag for a glowing, festive effect.

• Cut a bag open and glue on bright papers or other decorations, or paint on brown paper to create decorative wrapping paper.

• Use the bag "as is" decorating it using ideas such as animal characters, a particular holiday or party theme. Make any simple cut-out prints or use markers or paint to stencil on a pattern. Cut up old greeting cards for collage design. Or just cover a bag with scrap fabric patches or glue brightly colored yarn around it.

• Make a quick "gift" bag. Close a bag by folding over the top, punching holes in the top area and putting ribbon or yarn through the holes. Tie to close.

In college we'd use opened brown paper bags to "paper" people's doors shut from the hallway as a gag. When they'd open their doors, they would have to "break through" the wall of paper to leave the room.

Anonymous

KID STUFF

Go Fly A Kite

• Let kids decorate a small paper bag, using crayons and markers, to make a kite. Then, punch a hole on the top side of the bag near the opening, pull a piece of yarn through the hole (good idea to reinforce the hole with tape) and tie it. The kite will fill with air and fly when the kids run with it.

• Make a large streamer kite by folding over the top edge of a brown paper grocery bag to form a cuff. Glue long crepe paper streamers under the cuff and near the bottom of the bag. Punch two holes near the open end, reinforcing them to strengthen the paper. Put a long piece of string or yarn through the holes and knot it and let the kids run with it.

It's Academic!

• Make sturdy book covers from brown paper grocery bags. Cut off the bottom of the bag, then cut the bag open along the seam. Lay the book open on the paper and trace along the top and bottom of the book. Remove the book and fold down along lines you've traced. Place the book back on the paper, then fold over each side of the paper ends to form flaps (not longer than three inches) and insert front and back book cover into these flaps. Write school subject on the outside paper, or decorate, or just leave plain and use for doodling.

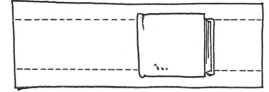 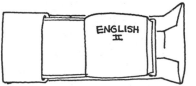

Party Time

• Have a large bag ready during a party (or the holiday season) for saving ribbons and bows as presents are being opened. Turn the top edges down about an inch to form a "collar" and the bag will stand open on its own.

• Design your own piñata. Decorate a large, paper grocery bag (don't use a double-strength one) using markers, stickers, streamers and cut paper. Leave three inches by the open end undecorated. At the top of the piñata, punch two holes on opposite sides. Thread a three-foot-long string through one hole and out the other. Knot the ends together. Fill the piñata with treats and small toys. Use old newspaper as excess filler. Close the open end of the piñata, fold it down and staple it closed. (The bottom of the bag will be the top of the piñata.) Hang by a secure string and let the kids swing away with a broom handle or bat.

- Open bags along seams so they lay flat and let kids at a party decorate the paper with crayons, markers, stamps, stickers, paint and sponge or hand prints to create cute gift wrap. The paper can be personalized with the gift-receiver's name or interests: cut into squares that kids can take home as favors.

Emotional Outlets
- Blow up a paper lunch bag. Hold it shut with one hand and smash both hands together for a big bang. It's a great emotional outlet for a kid. (Actually, it's good for grown-ups, too!)

Physical Outlets
- Keep a few excess paper bags handy in the car to use as good, impromptu barf bags.

> *My kids mainly used brown paper grocery bags as their "suitcases" when moving between our homes during their joint custody years. I hated seeing that. They had better carryalls and they had things at each house. I suspect that it meant changing houses wasn't such a major shift to them if they could throw what they needed in a paper bag.*
>
> *Marni Scott, Barrington, MA*

PAPER BAG ART

The brown paper bag has even taken its place as an art form today. This ranges from the simple—such as some of the ideas in this book—to the sophisticated. For instance, the Paper Bag Players, a theater group in New York City, began in 1958 and is still active today. Paper bags and boxes are used for all sets, props and costumes. The theater is about the art of transforming a paper bag into, as they say, "something magical!"

Some have utilized the decorative and tough qualities of paper bags to transform walls and even floors into interesting, textured surfaces. We'll leave that type of interior decorative art to the professionals, however.

Life-size Body Art

• Make personalized body drawings of your children. Cut open and tape together some brown grocery bags—enough so that the paper is a little bit wider and longer than the child. Have your child lie down on the paper and trace around his or her body with a pencil. Cut out the shape. Now you or your child can draw on it, dress it, or use cut-out pictures from magazines that you glue in place to create a portrait.

Masks and Costumes

Masks out of brown paper bags are easy and fun to make. They can be fearsome or friendly, happy or sad. Kids love the chance to let their imaginations wander. The adult can mark and cut eye and mouth holes in the bag in the appropriate spots by having the bag "tried on." Place your fingers where your mouth and eyes are and mark. Cut the bag off at the neck, or cut curved slots around the shoulders or holes for the placement of the child's arms. Then let kids go at it. If they need suggestions, mention a clown, a frog, a cat, or a bearded man. Use two bags for older, taller kids. To join, trim edges and cut bottom off one bag (you should have about an inch of overlap), glue or tape edges together, then continue.

• Make a "fluffy head" for your child, using a brown paper bag. Place bag over child's head and mark eyes and armholes with a felt pen. Remove bag and cut out the holes for eyes and arms. Place cotton balls (you'll need about two bags) into a saucer of diluted white glue and stick each one onto the bag, covering as much of the bag as you can. (You can scrunch pieces of tissue paper into balls and glue them on top for ears, or elsewhere, to cover gaps among cotton balls.)

- Turn a brown paper bag into a space walker mask or TV screen mask. Draw a large square with rounded corners in the face area and cut it out. Cover the face hole area with a clear acetate sheet from an office supply store, but cut out a center area to allow for air. Draw dials below and add any other appropriate details.

- Make dogs, cats, horses or lions from a brown paper grocery bag for Trick or Treating. For a one-piece costume, cut out arm holes (leave room for a bulky sweater) and eye holes. Children can decorate the bag themselves or with a parent's help. For a two-piece costume, cut out armholes and a neck hole in one bag and use a smaller one for the face mask.

- Let youngsters help create a clock or a playing card from a bag that fits them, with holes for head and arms.

Halloween Fun

- For party favors, centerpieces or hand-outs, fold the top half of a brown paper bag down and inside. With staples or tape, attach one piece of double-folded white, black or orange tissue paper to each side of the bag. Fill with goodies, then gather the tissue paper at the top and tie with a bright ribbon.

- Turn a flashlight into something special for Halloween by cutting out a "pumpkin face" from the bottom of a lunch bag and placing it over the light area of the flashlight.

- Make goody bags from brown paper lunch bags spooked-up with bats you make from black adhesive paper. Cut these out and stick "bats" on the paper bags. Color bats' eyes with white pencil or correction fluid. Stuff bags with black and orange tissue paper and fill with favors.

- Turn brown bags with handles into special trick-or-treat totes. Making your own bag allows you to truly coordinate a costume. Decorate with tempera paint, crayons, felt-tip markers, glitter or stickers, or motifs you sponge-paint on. Draw or glue on cutouts of ghosts, witches, cats and bats, a haunted house, monsters and skeletons. (Cotton makes great eyebrows, mustaches and animal fur, and buttons can be used for eyes and ears.)

- Or make your own "handled" bag by following this drawing:

Building Blocks

- Use paper bags to make big building blocks for forts, castles, towers and tunnels. Lay the bag flat on the floor or a low table. Fold the top over about six or eight inches and crease the bag on the fold. Open the bag and fill it with scrunched up newspapers, putting in one sheet at a time. Fold the bag on the crease line and securely tape it closed.

- Create a Paper-Bag City using a stack of stuffed, paper lunch bags. Decorate with crayons or markers to make doors and windows. Stand some horizontally and some vertically. With clear tape, attach one to another for stability.

Thanksgiving Gobblers

• Create a paper bag turkey by first stuffing the bottom of a brown lunch bag with scrunched up newspaper and twisting the top of that bag to form a long, skinny neck. Glue (or draw) googly eyes on to the bottom stuffed area (the head) and let an uninflated red balloon hang under the nose area. For the turkey's body, first snip a hole in the front of a regular brown paper grocery bag an inch from the bottom and pull the "neck" into the larger bag. Stuff the bag almost full of scrunched newspaper, then close the top of it with a rubber band. Make tail feathers by cutting four large half-circles from another brown bag and gluing them in layers to the "back of the body," covering the rubber-banded, closed part of the bag.

Create a Broom Cover

• Create a "Broom Friend" from a brown paper grocery bag. Turn the bag bottom-side-up and paint a face on one side. Now, wrap the bottom of the broom with newspaper. Place it all in the bag. Add more newspaper to fill out the "head." Tie the bag closed. For hair, glue on strips cut from construction paper, ribbons or yarn. Add an old hat and a scarf for decoration. Adding a hanger below the neck would allow you to add a shirt or coat. You can also make one as a witch, a scarecrow, a monster or an animal

Make Your Own Pattern

• Recovering a lamp shade? Need a stencil? Use an opened paper bag to create the pattern you need.

Puppetry

Children can make hand puppets out of brown paper lunch bags (the mouth is the fold at the bottom of the bag.) To make the "mouth" move, kids put their fingers inside the flap and move it up and down.

Decorative details can be painted, glued or taped on. This includes ribbon, yarn, buttons, lace, glitter—anything you have around the house. Soft pom-poms or cotton balls make good animal noses. A partially-inflated balloon can make a clown nose—or a tongue when placed in the fold/mouth of the bag. Create ears by cutting out the appropriate shapes from another bag, or colored paper, then taping them in place. An owl just needs googly eyes and a scrap of felt for a beak. Cover the balance of the bag with feathers, real or drawn on with markers.

Help your child make a Bunny Bag. Make a V-shaped cut at the top of a brown paper bag to form ears. Then, either you or the kids can cut a nose, whiskers and inner ears out of construction paper and glue them on. (Or kids can draw these on.) Glue a cotton ball tail to the back side and your bunny is complete.

Paper Crafts

• Use strips of brown grocery bags for creating small weaving projects. Cut two-inch wide strips, then fold and glue the edges under to make a finished strip about an inch wide. The strips form the basis for any type of woven design.

• Attractive—even classy—paper beads for stringing into various pieces of jewelry can be made from cut-up brown paper bags. Roll strips of paper width-wise and into varied thicknesses. You can roll the piece of paper around a straw or a string. After the strips are pasted closed and dried, they can be painted. Once dry, cut into various lengths and string for bracelets, necklaces and the like. (Longer, thick, unpainted tubes made from brown paper can be used to create mini log cabin structures.)

• Make a string of gingerbread men by cutting a long strip from a brown paper grocery bag and folding it like an accordion. Draw one-half of a gingerbread man, with hands and feet touching the folds, on the top. Cut out the shape, being careful not to cut through the folded parts at hands and feet. Obviously, other designs can be created this way, too.

• Use sections cut from paper bags to create a forest of small, brown trees. Cut same-size, large rectangular pieces of paper. Begin rolling one into another, with approximately four inches lead each time, into a roll or tube shape. At one end, cut down the tube about six inches, as many cuts as you can, spacing the cuts about one-half to one inch apart. Place your finger down this cut end of the tube and pull out the center paper and your tree's "leaves" will appear.

Burnished Metallic Finish

Glue several layers of brown kraft paper (cut from bags) together for a craft project of your choice. "Paint" the outer layers, front and back, with white or tacky glue. When dry, "burn" this outer glue carefully *(very carefully)* over a candle flame until the paper surface is covered with the soot of the flame. When cool, rub the surface with a rag or paper towel and a shiny, metallic surface will appear.

PAPER SHOPPING BAGS

Merchandise paper bags, known simply as "shopping bags"—those wonderful durable paper bags with sturdy handles—make up another part of the paper bag landscape. While some do come in the plain, brown variety, the ones distributed by retailers often tend to be more sophisticated and upscale. They're usually made of finer paper and advertise the company that gives them out, and they come in various sizes. Shopaholics usually have a good supply on hand. Today, they are even collectibles, as is evidenced by the book on the subject, SHOPPING BAG SECRETS by Sue Weiner and Fran Michelman (Universe Press, 1999). Obviously, the more high end the company (Chanel, Tiffany's, Dior), the more prestige the bag carries.

Store a large collection by putting the handles of several bags over the head of a hanger in a closet to keep them under control.

As the shopping bag has become an acceptable form of gift wrap, it has become a large category unto itself in paper and gift stores. The choices available truly boggle the mind. Today, you're bound to find a lovely bag in any color and any pattern to fit any occasion.

Collectible or not, you'll find one size or another handy to:

• Substitute for laundry baskets or hampers.

• Use to tote your laundry to and from the machines.

• Store newspapers for recycling.

• Store linen sets, standing on a closet shelf.

• Hold a specific outfit's accessories, hung conveniently on that outfit's hanger.

• Place on the floor for an instant cat toy!

• Store less attractive brown garbage bags.

• Use for holding and organizing shoe boxes.

• Make attractive, affordable floral table decorations. Hide a glass jar in a small or medium-sized bag, add water and fresh flowers, and…voila! A centerpiece!

• Save really pretty gift shopping bags to use in place of gift wrap for presents. After inserting the gift item, stuff some tissue or shredded colored paper on the top to cover the item. *NOTE:* Try not to give a gift bag back to the person who gave it to you!

Chapter Three

PLASTIC BAGS

The plastic bag has become an indispensable part of our lives. And its uses—and reuses—are limited only by imagination and lifestyle. I've now seen plastic bags that are actually hanging file folder bags. The top closure is a plastic snap-lock top that fits file drawers and the hanging file is clear plastic. You'll find bulk mail too, that comes in clear, bag "envelopes," as well as magazines.

Despite the variations in sizes, consumer options for plastic bags come in two major closing types: *resealable tops (zipper closing and slider locking)* or *open-ended tops*, and in two common weights or thicknesses: *freezer weight* or *other-than-freezer weight*.

Plastic storage and freezer bags are *not* designed to withstand the heat of boiling water. Storage and freezer bags (versus thin sandwich bags) can be used for defrosting and reheating foods in a microwave but be sure the bag is open or vented.

Although resealable bags are latecomers to the storage story, they have become the more important because of their convenience. Whether to keep things airtight or just to prevent spilling out, resealable bags work well in a good many places.

The latest variation of the resealable bag has a slide locking plastic tab for closure. For both the very young and the old and also those with motor control problems or poor small motor skills or joint problems, this type of bag has brought new independence.

The traditional paper lunch bag now has a plastic counterpart. Then there are the long, narrow bags used to deliver newspapers in many parts of the country, which have become a familiar part of our plastic landscape. Even if we don't include dry cleaning bags, the plastic bag in all its various sizes and weights impacts us daily. Retailers use plastic bags as cheap, disposable carry-alls, available in a large variety of sizes, and suitable for delivering various commercial messages. These take up far less storage room than their paper shopping bag counterparts, weigh less for shipping and cost the retailer less. The most popular style is known as the handled or T-bag plastic carryall. But, these bags, handy as they might be, create their own storage and disposal issues.

The ideas in this book for use and reuse of plastic bags are *not* organized by type of bag but, rather, by area of usefulness. Many tips indicate "resealable," but the type you choose to use is your decision. Some situations lend themselves to one type more than another. Many regular storage bags can be sealed with a twist-tie or clip and work as well as those with resealable tops. The variations in plastic bags that you can buy are truly multiple. For the moment, descriptions include: sandwich, storage, pint, quart, gallon, two gallon jumbo, vegetable, pleated bottom, fold-and-close top, snack, resealable, drawstring, trash, tall kitchen, lawn, freezer-weight and heavy duty freezer-weight. And who knows what will appear on the shelf next week!

Wretched Excess

Store excess plastic grocery bags in an empty tissue box, the cardboard core from paper towels or any sort of plastic bottle with the top cut off for a hole to stuff bags in. (You can cut another small hole at the bottom to pull out the bags you wish to use.) Or, a dozen bags rolled up tightly fit into a small, self-closing bag. And, of course, any other plastic bag can be used to hold extras. If you can't reuse them fast enough, drop your excess off in your grocery store's plastic collection container and keep them from the trash heap, where their demise WON'T be imminent.

IN THE KITCHEN

Food Preparation
• Help fruit to ripen faster by putting it in a plastic bag (or special perforated plastic bag) along with ripe fruit. The ripe fruit gives off a natural gas that speeds up the ripening process.

- Substitute plastic bags for bowls to mix dry ingredients or to thoroughly blend messy ones like those for meat loaf, meatballs or bread dough, pancake mix and even tuna salad. The best part is that you toss out the bag when you're through. Keep any printing on the outside, and consider lining one flimsy bag with another.

- Use a plastic bag, preferably a heavy duty one, to make a funnel to move ingredients from a larger to a smaller container. Just clip one corner of the filled bag and insert it into the larger container. You can also use this method in areas of the house other than the kitchen.

- Crack eggs into a self-sealing bag, close carefully and shake, shake, shake for scrambled eggs without an extra dish to clean. Easy enough for kids to do, too.

- Use a resealable bag as a strainer. Put into the bag whatever food item you're straining, then poke holes in the bag with a clean pin to create drainage.

- Stuff a bird the easy way by putting the prepared stuffing in a plastic bag, inserting the open end into the bird and squeezing the stuffing out. You won't lose a crumb.

- Prepare turkey in advance by deboning a cooled bird and storing it (sliced or in quarters) with a cup or two of chicken broth in a heavy-duty resealable bag in the fridge or the freezer.

- Use a handled, plastic grocery bag as a salad spinner. After washing greens, shake them over the sink to get rid of excess water. Put a dish towel in the bottom of the bag, place greens inside, then whirl the bag around until the contents are dry. (Some say this will take 10 "whirls.")

> *Self-closing bags are not only good for food, but for safety, too. Fill sandwich-size bags with baking soda. Keep one by the stove, at least one in your vehicle and one in your workshop. Presto. You have an inexpensive and effective fire extinguisher, should the need arise. It works!*
>
> *Harold Kaplan, Brooklyn, NY*

Keeping it Fresh

• Grate foods such as stale bread or cheese INSIDE a large, clear plastic bag. Grating and storing become a one-step process. And, stored in a plastic bag, grated cheese stays moist and fresh longer.

• Keep bread fresh longer by storing it in a tightly-closed plastic bag with a stalk of celery.

• Store packaged salad mix in self-closing bags in the fridge after opening to keep it fresher longer. Roll or squeeze out excess air before closing.

• Place an open, unfinished can of soda pop in a zip-top bag to keep it from going flat too quickly.

• Refrigerate artichokes for up to a week in a plastic bag to which you've added a few drops of water.

• Put cheese coated with butter in a zip-top bag and store it in the fridge to keep it from getting moldy. Or store and seal leftover pieces of cheese in an airtight plastic bag with a couple of cubes of sugar. Hard cheese will stay fresh for months.

• Store washed and drained salad greens in the refrigerator, with a paper towel, in a freezer-weight bag. Make sure all the air is squeezed out and the bag is sealed tightly.

- Make up at least two meal servings of salad from fresh produce and store the second one—minus dressing—in a self-closing bag for a next day's "instant" salad.

- Take the cooled broth from a roasted turkey and store it in a zip-top freezer bag. When it cools enough so that the fat congeals at the top of the bag, snip off a small, bottom corner for the clear broth to drain into your saucepan. Use for making fat-free gravy—especially good for mashed potatoes.

- Open large boxes and bags of snacks after grocery shopping and transfer the contents to zip-top bags to keep them fresh, or make individual snack bags for the kids. Small children can then choose a bag when they want a snack. (Many dieters say that portioning out snacks into bags ahead of time allows them to eat just one healthy serving size at a time rather than accidentally finishing off an entire box or bag of munchies.)

- Or put the whole open box that is stored in the pantry in a large,self-closing bag. It keeps the contents fresh, yet visible.

Great for fresh Parmesan cheese that I grate onto everything! I just keep a block in the bag and remove it to use every day. I don't have to keep re-wrapping it in plastic wrap and it keeps it nice and fresh for weeks.

Joana R. Gribko, Vienna, VA

Coffee, Spice and (keeping) Everything Nice
- Grind different flavors of coffee and store in separate, labeled bags in fridge or freezer.

- Preserve herbs from your garden through the winter. Package them in small, labeled plastic bags in your freezer. Keep them handy by clipping them to an inside shelf.

• Make bread crumbs quickly and neatly from boxed croutons by placing them in a heavy-duty plastic bag and smashing or rolling them into crumbs with a rolling pin, long bottle or the flat side of a meat tenderizer. Store any extra crumbs in a plastic bag in the freezer. (Do the same for making graham cracker or cookie crumb crusts.)

• Store dry products such as beans, rice or flour in plastic bags after opening, to cut down mess on cupboard shelves. Or, if you have problems with bugs or humidity, store in a plastic bag *inside* a canister.

Baking Tricks
• Keep a plastic sandwich bag in a can of vegetable shortening and use it like a mitten when you need to grease a pan.

• Put all the dry ingredients for a pie crust in a plastic bag, add water and seal or tie the bag tightly. Gently squeeze until the contents are thoroughly blended. Store the dough in the refrigerator until you're ready to roll it out.

• Spray the inside of a large, self-closing bag with a nonstick vegetable spray, put bread dough inside and place in a warm spot to rise.

• Put cookie dough and a few drops of food coloring in a self-closing bag and knead to mix thoroughly. (Your hands won't get dyed in the process.) You can make several packages of different colors and store in fridge or freezer to have available whenever you need them—especially helpful at holiday time.

• Store empty margarine wrappers from sticks, with excess margarine still attached, in self-closing bags in the fridge or freezer. When you need to grease a pan or cookie sheet, just take out one of the wrappers.

- Put a small amount of chocolate (or a few chocolate chips) in a freezer-weight, zip-top bag in hot water—not boiling—and, when melted, cut a small piece off the corner of the bag and squeeze out soft chocolate for cake decorating.

- Keep brown sugar soft and usable by storing it in a freezer-weight, zip-top bag in the refrigerator.

- Consider using bags to make candy, such as fudge. While the candy is still warm and soft, place it in a self-closing bag, release excess air, close bag, press candy out flat to fit the bag, then open bag and allow candy to cool. After it's cool, slide it out of the bag, cut into pieces, then replace it in the bag and close. No pans to wash and the candy is in an airtight container. You could even give this away as a gift if you put a bow or other decoration on the bag.

- Keep homemade soft cookies fresh for a long time in zip-top bags. Want them really soft? Add a slice of bread to the bag.

- Freeze already-baked cookies, waiting to be iced or decorated, and take them out during summer vacation when kids are bored and looking for something to do.

- Create a festive look when giving gift cookies out in zip-top bags by inserting a piece of solid color paper—cut to fit the bag—to "match" the holiday. It could also have the recipe on it.

COOKING IN BAGS

Oven bags—which are not plastic, but heat-resistant nylon—are wonderful for roasting meat and poultry. They keep in the moisture and minimize pan clean-up. You can also use an oven bag inside a crockpot. It's easy because there is nothing to clean after you lift the bag and all the ingredients from the pot.

Food for a Crowd

• Freeze water in a deep dish pie plate and transfer it to a clear plastic bag. Then, keep a plate of cold foods chilled, at a dinner or party, by placing the plate on top of the bag.

• Fill a plastic bag with your party punch and freeze to form a block of "ice." Use the block in your punch bowl, so that it stays cold, but doesn't get diluted.

• Put vegetable salad makings for a big crowd into a clean eight-gallon trash bag and pour the dressing in. Secure the open end of the bag, then turn it over several times to toss before filling—and refilling—the salad bowl.

• Use plastic bags to give company leftovers from dinner, instead of giving them your favorite containers that you may never see again.

Chop, Mix and Marinate

• Chop nuts in a self-closing freezer bag, after excess air has been squeezed out, using a rolling pin or heavy bottle or can to crush them. You can see when they're the right size and leftovers can be stored in the bag.

• Use a zip-top bag to mix such ingredients as the stuffing for deviled eggs or icing for decorating cakes and cookies. Mix the food, seal the bag, cut a corner off and use like a pastry tube to squeeze the stuffing out. For icing, place different colors in separate pint-size bags. You can also put different colors of decorating sugar in bags pierced with fork tines to sprinkle on cakes or cookies.

• Marinate meat or poultry in a large, self-closing freezer bag. Place the marinade ingredients directly in the bag, close it and shake to mix. Then add meat, press out any excess air in the bag and reseal it. Place it in the refrigerator and turn the bag occasionally. If meat won't be used by the next day, place the bag, as is, in the freezer.

• Marinate and store beef jerky in zip-top bags.

Place flour and seasonings in a self-closing bag. Then add chops or chicken and close. Turn bag over to coat items, before cooking.
Frida Keane, Surrey, CO

Outdoor Cooking

• Store spices and utensils for outdoor cooking in self-closing bags.

• Bring 'marinated-in-the-bag' meats and poultry right to the grill in the bag.

• Protect your barbecue grill by covering it with a large, heavy-duty trash bag, but cover it only after it's cooled.

Holding Power

• Hang plastic grocery bags on the inside of a kitchen cabinet or pantry to collect aluminum cans for recycling.

• Hang a handled, plastic grocery bag inside a cabinet to collect the plastic bags that you take back to the supermarket for recycling.

• Tape plastic sandwich bags to the inside of a lower kitchen cabinet door to hold rubber bands, twist ties, paper clips and such.

• Place a magnet inside a small, open bag and keep it *ON* the refrigerator door to keep coupons, UPCs and rebate forms.

Contain Yourself

- Some folks suggest storing a box of resealable bags *RIGHT IN* the fridge. This can be helpful when you're putting away left-overs after a big meal or for kids, as a reminder.

- Turn less expensive storage plastic bags, including sandwich-size ones, into "dish covers" by sliding dishes right into them when putting items in the refrigerator, rather than using plastic wrap.

- Store small amounts of leftover food in self-closing bags, rather than in plastic containers, to save space. (Cool hot foods before placing in bags.)

Transporting deviled eggs to potluck suppers? Place the egg white halves to be filled on serving dish and cover securely. Put all the filling into the self-closing bag, press out most of the air and zip closed. When you get to the serving area, snip a small hole in a lower corner of the self-closing bag and fill the deviled eggs as if you were using a pastry bag. Dust with paprika to garnish. No more deviled eggs' tops stuck onto the serving dish covering!
Katy Manck, Gilmer TX

Traveling with Food

- Make a portable salad. Put salad dressing in a small zip-top bag and, when ready to eat, snip a small hole in the bottom corner of the bag and squeeze the dressing onto your salad. Particularly good for picnics and pot luck parties, but also for brown bag lunches. Or, do the same with condiments-to-go, such as ketchup and mustard.

- Use bread bags to carry sandwiches, individually wrapped or not.

- If you have to prepare a meal in a strange kitchen, such as a church or a friend's or relative's house, do the "prep" work at home (chopping onions and such) and bring the ingredients in zippered bags. Usually, it's quicker, easier and less frustrating to do most things in your own kitchen.

• Keep lettuce fresh and crispy for a sandwich you've packed for lunch. Wrap it in a paper towel and put it in a separate, small plastic bag. Add it to the sandwich when you're ready to eat.

• Bring plastic bags along to a pot luck dinner to carry home any dirty utensils or containers.

Getting the Air Out

To prevent freezer burn, get as much air as possible out of the filled plastic bag before sealing. Squeeze out air by:

1) rolling bag to remove excess air and then sealing it shut,

   or by

2) sucking the air out by inhaling at a small opening. Another way to accomplish this is to insert a straw in the bag, then zip it closed as far as it will go and inhale the air through the straw. In one quick motion, remove the straw and zip or slide the bag closed,

   or by

3) placing an open, resealable bag with liquid ingredients upright in a narrow container when removing excess air. It allows both hands to be free as you work the air out of the bag, making freezing liquids a spill-free operation.

Remember when freezing liquids to allow an inch or two of space at the top of the freezer bag, since liquids expand when frozen.

Luscious Leftovers

• Make lots of soup, then freeze leftovers in family-size portions in bowls. When they are frozen, remove the rounds and place them in freezer bags.

• Turn back the top of a bag as you put leftovers inside to keep top and "zipper" area clean.

• Take advantage of two-for-one pizza deals on take-out pizza even if you don't have a big family. Order both pizzas, eat one and freeze the other, in a zip-top bag, of course.

• Freeze leftover buttermilk in 1/2 cup measures in zip-top bags. For convenient storing, gather the small bags into a larger one after freezing. Thaw in the microwave when needed.

• Put leftover heavy cream in one-ounce paper cups, cover and place in zip-top freezer bags. When you're ready to use it, defrost partially and whip it up.

• Stock up on bananas when they're on sale. Allow them to ripen (if not already ripe), then peel and freeze in zip-top bags and they're ready to use for all your banana favorites from bread to frozen bananas on-a-stick or fruit drinks.

Makin' It Easy

• Place slices or scoops of ice cream in zip-top sandwich bags in the freezer so kids can serve themselves or anyone can easily make root beer floats.

• Make ahead and freeze Hollandaise sauce to avoid last-minute panic. Thaw by running warm water over the bag.

• Make lots of pasta sauce. Allow it to cool, then put one-meal portions in zip-top bags and freeze. Just heat and eat when you're ready.

- Bake a few extra biscuits, fill each with a piece of sausage and zip closed. Freeze for quick, microwave treats.

- Soften dried-out marshmallows by sealing them in a zip-top bag and immersing the bag in a pan of hot (not boiling) water for a few minutes.

I love using self-closing bags to make hamburger patties. Just drop in a ball of burger, close bag and press it flat. Stack them in the freezer.

Jackie Dodge, Newport, WA

Kids in the Kitchen
- If your young cooks don't like getting their hands sticky when they help you cook, let them wear plastic bags on each hand to knead doughs, mix meat loaves or grease pans. This works for big cooks, too!

- Put 1/2 cup milk, 1 tablespoon sugar and 1/4 teaspoon vanilla in a quart-size bag, press the air out and seal. Put that bag, along with a cup or two of salt (rock salt, if available) and lots of ice, in a gallon-size bag. Squeeze the air out and seal. Wrap in paper towels to protect hands from the cold. Roll it back and forth on a hard surface for about five minutes. When it gets to be ice cream, eat it!

Kids on the Run
- Put snacks for children, in portioned servings, in zip-top bags on a low shelf in your refrigerator, so kids know where to find them and can help themselves. Keep bunches of washed grapes in bags, so kids can grab a nourishing snack for eating on-the-run or putting in a school lunch.

- Keep kids' half-eaten or sucked-on food in zip-top bags in the fridge or freezer for them to finish later.

- Keep some seedless grapes in a plastic snack bag in the freezer for a delicious, on-the-run or eat-in-the-car crunchy snack.

- Freeze a flavored drink and a CLEAN, small toy (small enough to fit in the bag, but not small enough to be swallowed) in a small, resealable bag. Cut a lower corner off and kids can suck the drink out as it melts. (This can be messy. Save it for an out-door treat.) When they're finished, kids can claim their "prize."

I use self-closing bags for storing baked, ready-to-decorate Christmas cookies in the freezer. When the weather is frightful, I pull a bag of cookies out of the freezer and set the kids up at the kitchen table with frosting and decorations (stored in self-closing bags, of course.) It's an activity that keeps them happy and occupied and gets them away from the TV and video games for quite awhile.

Sharon E. Mannix, Windsor, NY

Freezing Cold

- Store excess ice cubes in plastic bags in the freezer and they won't stick together.

- Accordion-pleat waxed paper and insert a strip of bacon in each fold. Place carefully in a self-closing bag and freeze.

- Put an opened container of ice cream in a resealable bag to keep ice crystals from forming on it.

All Thumbs in the Grocery Store

To open plastic bags in those continuous rolls in the produce department, wet your finger and thumb, grasp the end of the bag between them, rub your fingers back and forth and the bag edges will separate. To grab that produce, put your hand in the bag and grasp item, pull the bag over your hand and food item and you have "bagged" it with minimal effort.

Fruits and Vegetables

• Freeze apples for baking uses by peeling, coring, slicing and blanching them in boiling water for two minutes. Cool in ice water, then drain and freeze in bags.

• Freeze a cored, washed and dried head of cabbage in a zip-top bag and you will not be troubled by the characteristic strong odor when you cook it. The cabbage will soften quickest when it is boiled. (You can freeze just the outer leaves, boil them briefly and use them for making stuffed cabbage rolls.)

• Grate a large batch of carrots at the same time and freeze recipe-size amounts in plastic bags. Good for carrot salad, cake, muffins and such. They'll thaw in the preparation process.

Occasionally, there is a really good sale on bananas. When that happens, I load up and set them out to ripen. I then peel and freeze them in self-closing bags. I now have a few weeks' supply of banana-sicles for my kids (and myself) who love them. It sure is more nutritious than popsicles.

Nancy Resnick, Seattle, WA

Tray Freezing

You can freeze the following foods best in single layers on a tray or cookie sheet first, so they will be separate till they're hardened; then transfer to resealable freezer bags, and the pieces will not adhere to each other.

◻ Tomato paste, in one-tablespoon amounts
◻ Minced garlic, in 1/2 teaspoon amounts
◻ Berries (do not wash first) and grapes, in a single layer, or any favorite fruits in bite-size pieces
◻ Asparagus and other delicate vegetables (blanch by steaming or submerging in water for a few minutes, then drain)
◻ Scoops of leftover whipped cream
◻ Leftover pancakes or waffles (with waxed paper between)

¤ Frosted cupcakes or decorated cookies (transfer to freezer bags after frosting is hard)

¤ Unbaked cookies (add about 2 minutes to your baking time when baked straight from the freezer)

¤ Bacon, either cooked slices or crumbled pieces

We use self-closing bags to freeze punch. When the punch is ready to serve, we have eliminated the need for ice, which waters down the punch, and added only the punch flavor.
Sharon O'Brien, St. Louis Park, MN

Freeze the following foods in a molded ice cube tray, then bag for future use:

¤ fresh-squeezed lemon or lime juice, leftover lemon- or limeade, or any kind of fruit juice

¤ leftover coffee

¤ honey

¤ gravy

¤ spaghetti or pizza sauce

¤ chicken stock

¤ pan juices from meat

¤ puréed vegetables

¤ herbs (clean and chop herbs, put a tablespoon into each compartment, cover with water and freeze)

¤ onions (chop fine in blender or processor with a little water)

¤ homemade baby food (when frozen, store two cubes to a small bag. When it's feeding time, take out a bag and defrost the contents or heat in hot water. Then, cut off a corner and squeeze into a bowl. Or store all frozen cubes in a single large freezer bag and remove frozen cubes as needed. (For a more lengthy discussion of making baby food, read my book *FEED ME I'M YOURS.*)

Easy Freezin'

• Run blanched peeled or unpeeled tomatoes through a blender. Let sit for an hour or two. The water settles to the bottom and you can pour off the top concentrate and bag and freeze it for later use as a base for tomato soup, stews or sauces.

• Wash, dry and core tomatoes, then freeze them whole. Thaw in a bowl before using them for cooking. (Or dip in warm water for a few seconds, then peel.)

• Cover a pie tin with foil, pour in any leftover fruit pie filling, cover and freeze. Then, next time you make a crust you can just drop in your pie filling.

• Freeze turkey necks and giblets in a freezer bag for the next time you're making soup.

• Freeze freshly-caught fish in clean water by submerging the open bag (with the fish in it) in a sink or container of water while closing. The water will displace the air in the bag.

• Freeze the following foods in individual or recipe-size portions in zip-top freezer bags:
   ◻ hamburger patties, roasts, steaks, chops, chicken breasts and fish fillets (with plastic wrap between the pieces for quicker defrosting or individual use.)
   ◻ ground meat (press into a flat layer that fills the bag, squeezing out as much air as possible)
   ◻ washed, blanched, cooled and drained fresh vegetables
   ◻ day-old bread to use for French toast, bread pudding, croutons or bread crumbs.
   ◻ sautéed mushrooms
   ◻ shredded hard cheeses
   ◻ herbs (blanch basil for one minute and spread on paper towels till dry)
   ◻ leftovers such as pasta, meat loaf, chili, casseroles and soup

◘ sandwiches in sandwich-size bags, then gathered in a larger,
freezer bag. (Leave out non-freezeable ingredients such as
mayo or lettuce.) Try sliding sandwiches intact into the bag
on a pancake turner.

Baking Supplies You Can Keep Cool and Fresh in the Freezer

• Store whole wheat flour in a resealable bag in the freezer
to keep it from spoiling, if you won't use it up in eight
weeks.

• Cut the chilling time in half for dough that requires chilling by using flour you keep in the freezer.

• Keep whole or shelled nuts in the freezer for up to six
months or store toasted nuts for up to a month.

• Prevent bug infestation of a pastry cloth by rolling it in
a resealable bag and storing it in the freezer.

Clean & Neat

• Clean cooled oven racks or grill racks by placing them in a large
size, heavy-duty plastic garbage bag with enough full-strength
ammonia to cover them. Seal the bag with a tie and set it aside
(preferably outdoors) for several hours or overnight. If you don't
like to use ammonia, vinegar will work, too, but not quite as
well. Do clean-up outside with a hose, if possible, or in a laundry sink inside. Direct bag opening away from you when opening it. Use the same method to clean grill 'rocks' also, but check
the instruction manual first.

• Clean precious silver by slipping your hands into plastic bags
and securing them at your wrists with rubber bands.

• Place soap-filled steel wool pads in bags to keep them rust-free and eliminate the soapy muck in the bottom of whatever holder you use. Put your hand in a sandwich-size plastic bag and grab the soap pad. Pull the pad into the bag, turning it wrong side out, and the pad is ready to store—and reuse. Or put the bag in the freezer to further minimize rust.

- Pick up a dropped egg with your hand, covered with a plastic sandwich bag.

- Keep small appliances (such as a hand mixer) clean, dry and dust-free by storing them in zip-top bags.

- Keep some small, plastic bags on hand to use if you need to pick up the phone quickly when your hands are greasy from cooking or dirty.

- To avoid staining your cookbook, place it—open to the page you're using—in a large plastic bag on the counter.

- Sprinkle a little baking soda in a resealable bag, then empty it out (so the bag is just "powdered') to store sterling silver items and help reduce tarnishing.

Trash It
- Save bread bags, produce bags or newspaper bags to be used as mini garbage bags. They are especially great for bones or wet garbage.

- After a large dinner gathering, line a large mixing bowl with a bag and scrape off plates into the bowl for quick and easy garbage disposal.

- Pour cooled cooking oil from fried foods in a used zip-top bag instead of pouring it into the sink when disposing of it. You'll keep your drains clog-free.

- Freeze food to be thrown away in an already-used, resealable bag until trash day to keep domestic animals out of the garbage can and eliminate bad smells in the house.

- Fill a small, resealable bag with potpourri and punch air holes in it. Tape it to the inside lid of your garbage or trash can to counteract kitchen smells.

HOUSEHOLD STRATEGIES

Closet Keepers

- Keep a large, handled plastic trash bag on a hanger in your closet. As you come across items you'll no longer wear, place them in the bag. When it's full, start another bag. You'll have everything ready for your garage sale or to donate to the rummage fund-raiser. Do the same in the kids' rooms, too.

- Use narrow newspaper bags to store out-of-season shoes and keep them clean and dust-free.

- Make a quick, inexpensive garment bag. Pull clothing items (on hangers) through the open end of a large trash bag. Then, poke the hangers through the bottom of the bag, which now becomes the top, and the bag slides over the clothes. Use smaller kitchen trash bags to cover hanging blouses, skirts and sweaters you want to keep dust-free.

- Save room in your closet by rolling skirts, covered in a plastic bag (even a dry cleaning bag) to prevent creasing, then storing them in a drawer.

- Store rolled-up sleeping bags in sturdy, lawn-size trash bags. Buy bags with drawstring handles–just pull the strings tight to close the bag.

- Keep everything you need for seldom-worn outfits in one place. Hang tux, suit or dress on a hanger, then put items such as cuff links, studs, collar stays or scarves, jewelry and evening purse in a resealable bag and attach to hanger.

> *I fill resealable bags with cedar chips. I use a paper punch to punch a couple of holes in each bag, near the bottom (to release the aroma) and punch one hole at the top, to slip over a wire hanger. I keep these "cedar sachets" in our closets and change them once each month. Keeps our closets smelling terrific!*
>
> *Connie L. Garlough, Springfield, OH*

Top Drawer!

- Store small items such as jewelry, hankies, lingerie, scarves, and gloves in separate zip-top bags and they'll be easy to find in your dresser drawer.

- Keep polished sterling silver jewelry tarnish-free by storing it in a resealable bag with excess air squeezed out.

- Store pantyhose in bags before putting them in a drawer to prevent them from snagging.

> *I organized my junk drawer. One [bag] for matches, one for pencils and pens, one for sample products. The drawer looks great. It was such a mess.*
>
> *Dena R. Farland, Marshalltown, IA*

Good Scents

- Put together your own herbal potpourri. Seal the following ingredients in a self-closing bag for a few weeks: cinnamon sticks, whole cloves and allspice berries, dried roses, tiny pinecones, strips of orange or lemon rind, juniper sprigs, bay leaves blended with orrisroot (available at your local crafts store) and a few drops of rose, cinnamon and balsam oils. Turn the bag occasionally. Place in an open bowl.

• Or transfer potpourri to small, self-sealing bags and poke holes in the bags with a small, pointy knife or toothpick and place in drawers or on closet shelves.

• Or put into a self-sealing bag potpourri that you've bought. Poke holes in the bag, then wrap in the fabric of your choice for a pretty sachet.

• Refresh potpourri (whether homemade or not) by putting scented oil in a self-sealing bag with it. Leave for at least 24 hours. Shake the bag occasionally. When opened, it will be re-scented.

• Retain the scent in your scented candles longer by storing them in zip-top bags.

• Store aromatherapy light rings in zip-top bags, since they tend to become sticky after continued use with essential oils.

• Store bath oil beads the same way, to keep them fresh and fragrant.

Shoes and Bags

• Use plastic bags over shoes, inside boots, to keep both shoes and feet dry in case the boots are not totally waterproof.

• Slip your hand into a small, plastic bag before cleaning or polishing sandals and avoid getting it messy with shoe polish or cleaning fluid.

• Stretch leather shoes by putting a freezer bag in each shoe. Pour enough water into the bags to fill the shoes, being sure to close the bags tightly so the water doesn't leak out. Then, put each shoe in another plastic bag, so the outside of the shoes is protected, and put the shoes in the freezer for twenty-four hours. As the water expands, the shoes will stretch. When you take them out of the freezer, they'll need to defrost for awhile before you'll be able to remove the plastic bags from the shoes.

• Stuff leather handbags and/or shoes with recycled plastic bags to help maintain their shape.

• Pack shoes for traveling in plastic storage bags so your clothes stay clean and odor-free.

• Use several small bags in your purse for keys, credit and business cards, hand cream, medications, contact lens case, etc., and keep everything clean and easy to pull out when you need it.

Line your potted plants with a self-closing bag so that when you water them, the water doesn't run out the bottom and make a mess.

Amy M. Briggs, Huntsville, AL

In the Laundry

• To smooth out wrinkles, put a large, clean garment bag over a hanger and place drip-dry garments *over* the bag. This gives more body shape and the garment won't cling to itself.

• Replace laundered cushion covers on foam cushions more easily by first enclosing the foam cushion in plastic from a dry cleaner's bag.

• If you go out to do laundry, first separate your loads at home, then measure the appropriate amount of detergent for each load into small, zip-top bags and enclose one (for transport, only) with each load. Use the premeasured detergent as you deal with each load. Save the bags to use the next time you do laundry. (Consider putting premeasured amounts of detergent in bags at home, so kids can easily do laundry. Do the same to take with you if you'll do laundry when traveling.)

• Keep a plastic bag hanging near your washing machine and use it to collect salvageable items you find in family members' pockets before laundering clothes.

• Store dryer sheets in a resealable bag and they will retain their scent longer. This will also keep the strong, flowery smell of the dryer sheets from permeating the area where they're stored.

• Punch a few small holes in the top half of a resealable bag, add liquid fabric softener and drop in your washing machine as a slow-release dispenser.

• Soak used dryer sheets in a resealable bag along with a capful of liquid fabric softener. After they've soaked for awhile, take them out, let them air dry and they'll be renewed.

> *I keep two plastic bags in the laundry room for 'orphan' socks from the dryer—one bag for light socks, one bag for dark. I sort through them periodically to find the mates.*
> *Donna A. Flenard, Hinsdale, IL*

Pressing Ideas

• Place dampened clothes in a plastic bag in the refrigerator or freezer when you can't iron them for 48 hours or longer. This is especially convenient for napkins and placemats, since you can pull them out and iron them as needed. Wrap colored and white clothes separately.

• Lightly sprinkle clothes to be ironed, put them in a plastic bag and microwave on High until warm to the touch (try one-half minute first), then iron right away. *(CAUTION: Be sure there are no metal parts on the clothing.)*

- Attach a plastic bag under your ironing board to hold pressing cloths, needle and thread (for quick repairs) and a small scissors for snipping loose threads. A small, handled bag works well here.

Bathroom Cleaning

- For a quick, no-mess toilet clean-up, put your hand in a plastic bag while you scrub with a cloth or sponge. When through, remove bag and discard it.

- Tie a plastic bag containing vinegar or descaler around your bathroom faucet or showerhead. Leave until the scale is dissolved, then rinse clean.

- Line your wastebasket with a plastic trash bag to make clean-up fast. Store extra bags at the bottom of any wastebasket you line and you'll always know where your next liner can be found. Or store the whole roll of trash bags at the bottom of the basket and under the bag you're using to save time and shelf space.

- Use a large, resealable plastic bag for cleaning hairbrushes. Put shampoo and brushes in, zip closed and soak.

> *My husband likes to watch TV while relaxing in the bathtub but he was leery of using the remote in case it got wet. We put it in a slide-locking plastic bag and now he doesn't worry.*
> *Kim Schiller, Minneapolis, MN*

Cleaning Quickies

- Secure the heads of sponge floor mops in plastic bags tied with a twist-tie so they won't dry out and warp when stored.

- Keep dusting cloths containing lemon or teak oil in zip-top bags to prevent hardening and drying out between use. Stored this way, they can be reused many times.

- Carry a handled bag for collected trash as you clean, moving from room to room. And carry another one for items that need to be returned to other rooms.

- Set the legs of chairs and other furniture pieces into sandwich bags when shampooing carpets to prevent rust marks on carpeting and to protect furniture from moisture.

Mattress Magic

- Waterproof a mattress by cutting open a large, plastic trash bag and placing it under the sheet.

- Slip plastic trash bags between the mattress and box spring, and you'll find turning the mattress easier.

I keep ear plugs in a self-closing bag next to my bed in case my honey's snoring is keeping me up. Also easy for my travel needs.
Amy Mook, Madison, WI

Home Helpers

- Line a box or basket with a folded plastic trash bag to use as a "boot keeper" by the door in wet or snowy weather.

- Wrinkle a plastic dry cleaner's bag slightly and place it under throw rugs on hardwood or asphalt tile floors to help prevent slips.

- Before filling your humidifier, insert a trash bag in the reservoir, fold the bag over the top rim (snip, if necessary, for the float), and you have a throw-away liner.

- Protect matches for the fireplace in self-closing bags.

- Place your TV remote in a self-closing bag to keep it safe from greasy fingers.

- Anticipating a power outage? Store water in large, resealable freezer-weight bags. If your water supply will be around more than a few days, add 1/2 teaspoon of chlorine to the large bag to keep the water quality safe or just plan on boiling the water before using it.

Repairing and (Re)Decorating

- When painting a room that has a ceiling fan in it, protect the fan blades by putting long, plastic bags over them, secured with masking tape.

- Protect hanging lamps and chandeliers from sanding dust and dripping paint. Release the cover plate that is screwed into the ceiling (save screws in resealable bag) and let it slide down the chain. Pull a dry cleaner's plastic bag up over the entire unit and tie it as high up on the chain as possible.

- If you can't finish a latex paint job in one work session, store the paintbrush or roller for several days by slipping it inside a plastic bag. Push excess air out and secure it shut, storing it overnight in the fridge.

- Keep leftover paint fresh by pouring it into a heavyweight, resealable plastic bag. Squeeze out the air and seal the bag. Put the bag in the original paint can and tape the lid closed.

- Put an item to be spray painted into a plastic shopping bag much larger than the item, then spray it. When dry, remove item and discard the bag.

• Use a sand-filled plastic bag as a weight to hold in place items you're repairing or working on when you've "run out of hands."

Economizing

• Buy household batteries when they're on sale and store them in the freezer in bags marked with the purchase date.

• Save soap slivers in a resealable or boil-in bag. When you have enough to make a new bar, heat in a pan on stove top over low heat until melted together. When the contents of the bag have cooled, you'll have a new block of soap.

• Store glycerin soap, whether for everyday or travel, in plastic bags because moisture will make this expensive but good-for-your-skin soap disintegrate very rapidly.

Storage Strategies

• Store hardware from bed frames or other furniture you've taken apart in resealable bags. Attach the bags to the furniture for quick assembly at the new location.

• Pack all the odds and ends from junk drawers and such in resealable bags.

• Separate hardware needed for hurricane shutters in bags and mark with the location of the shutters.

• Use large, resealable bags to store wool sweaters off-season. You'll know which sweater is enclosed and insects/moths won't be able to get in the bag.

• Use plastic bags to cushion breakable items when packing them for a move. Inflate the bag by blowing into it (after the small item is inside) then secure it shut.

In the Workshop/Garage

• Organize and store nuts, bolts, screws, washers, nails and drill bits in self-closing bags. Keep them rust-free and preserve the lubricant by putting a small amount of WD-40 in the bags. Hang the bags on a pegboard for easy spotting.

• Put tools in resealable bags with rust inhibiting chips for long-term storage.

• Store rolls of tape in resealable bags to keep them clean and easy to find.

• Put instruction books and warranties for outdoor or workshop equipment in a large, resealable bag and tack it to the wall in garage or workshop. Papers stay clean and dry; everything is handy in case you need it.

• Keep rags used for washing the car in self-closing bags, too.

At the Garage Sale...

• Gather such items as jewelry, hair accessories and small toys in plastic bags for your garage sale. A bag with one price on it will sell better than a bunch of loose items and you might avoid some theft.

• Keep some large-enough plastic bags on hand for folks to carry their treasures home .

• Cover paper advertising GARAGE SALE signs with a plastic storage bag or a dry cleaning bag in case it rains.

In the Garden

• Put leftover garden seeds in resealable bags, squeeze out air, seal shut, label and store in a cool, dry place till the next planting season.

- Germinate seeds by wrapping them in a moist paper towel and closing them up in a resealable bag. Store away from direct sunlight for a few weeks.

- Mix and store a planting mixture (potting soil, vermiculite and perlite) for household plants in a resealable bag.

- Store small lawn and flower bed supplies, such as a trowel or plant stakes, in self-closing bags. Slip the ends of other gardening tools in bags to help prevent rust.

- Use plastic bags as containers for plants to be transplanted, and cover small seedlings outdoors with bags to protect them from frost. Make sure to anchor the edges of the bags with dirt. Plants love the "greenhouse effect."

- Or use self-closing bags to grow seedlings. Tack bags up on a board. Put a little potting soil, water and seeds in each. They will grow...into "bag" gardens.

- Slip slider-closing bags over the fruit on trees while it ripens to keep insects from it.

- Store garden bulbs in vented vegetable bags until you're ready to plant them.

- Wrap the stems of just-picked flowers in a wet paper towel, place the stems in a resealable bag and seal the bag as far as possible around them.

- Save yourself the job of cleaning out a grungy flower vase (but not a clear glass one) by first inserting an appropriately-sized plastic bag, filled with water. Then, when you're ready to throw away the flowers, simply pull the whole thing out and discard.

- Cover your shoes with plastic bags, secured around the ankles, when working in a muddy garden.

> *Use resealable bags to propagate cuttings from plants that you want to replicate. Take cutting from plant. Dip end of the cutting into a rooting medium. Add some long grain sphagnum moss to bottom of bag. Tuck bottom of cutting into sphagnum moss. Zip bag and keep in warm place (not direct sunlight.) Wait. Then, watch cutting sprout. When it is big enough to pot, remove from self-closing bag and plant it, using your regular potting routine.*
> *Bonnie Madsen, St. Michael, MN*

Outside the House

• Cut large, used-but-clean trash bags into strips to use as stuffing for outdoor cushions.

• Clean gutters by lining a bucket with an appropriate-size plastic bag for your collection of leaves. Hook the bucket onto your ladder as you work along the edges of the gutter. Use a gloved hand or barbeque tongs to grad the leaves.

• Make a scarecrow by cutting a large trash bag into strips and stapling it to the top of a paper cup. Nail the cup to a tree or pole wherever you want to scare the birds away, and the blowing strips will do just that.

• Use plastic bags to protect outdoor water and gas valves in the wintertime.

KID STUFF

Babies On-the-Go

• Pack your baby's diaper bag with all the necessary supplies neatly organized in self-closing bags. Anything that can spill will be contained and it will all be ready to go when you are.

- Measure individual servings of formula into self-closing bags to carry in your diaper bag, instead of buying the premeasured packets. It's much cheaper and you can make them according to your needs.

- Use resealable bags to make ice packs for baby bottle carriers; seal ice in a bag, then put the ice pack inside the bottle bag.

- Put your toddler's training cup in a bag to take with you wherever you go. (Some "sippy" cups aren't completely spill-proof!)

- Keep extra plastic bags in your diaper bag and put dirty diapers in them to dispose of later if there's no convenient place to dispose of them at the time. At home, (or when visiting someone else's home) put dirty diapers into a bag before depositing in trash, so you don't have the odor in the house while waiting until the trash is put out.

- Put a wet washcloth in a resealable bag for quick clean-ups away from home. Carry it in your purse or glove compartment. Sprinkle in a bit of baking soda to keep the cloth smelling sweet.

- Use a large plastic bag as a diaper changing mat in an emergency. It's easy to carry with you.

Great for making baby wipes. I use the softest paper towels and put them in a self-closing bag with a small amount each of baby oil and antibacterial soap. Shake until towels are slightly damp. Works better than commercial wipes and stays moister than the wipes in the tubs.

Susan P. Marchman, La Crescenta, CA

Clothing
- Organize your baby's stored clothing by size in resealable bags.

• Let your kids dress themselves in the morning. Keep an outfit for each day (matching top and bottom, socks and underwear) in a large, zip-top bag.

WARNING
Never leave a small child unsupervised with any form of plastic bag. Put into a mouth or around a face, a plastic bag can easily cause suffocation.

Organizing Kid Stuff

• Store diaper wipes, once the box is opened, in a gallon-size resealable bag. They tend to dry out if left in the original box since it often doesn't close properly. (Also, toss a small, resealable bag of diaper wipes in your diaper bag when you're going somewhere.)

• Put bath toys in a large, plastic bag with a handle. Punch a few holes in the bottom for drainage—or try the new veggie aerated bags for small items. You can hang a large "vented" bag over a shower nozzle to drain.

• Store children's collections or treasures, especially those brought in from outside, in resealable bags.

• Pack up children's sandbox toys in a self-closing bag after they're finished playing. The toys will be kept together so children can find them next time they're ready to play.

• Store magnetic letters that kids play with on the refrigerator door in a resealable bag on top of the fridge. They'll be handy and gathered together when the kids want to play again.

• Place children's baby teeth in resealable bags. Kids can carry one around and show friends and neighbors without losing the tooth. The Tooth Fairy will be able to find a bag easily and can even leave the child's money in the bag.

• Keep puzzle and board game pieces (and their rules) and all those tiny parts to kids' toys in resealable bags.

• Use resealable plastic bags as goodie bags at children's birth-day parties, with each child's name on the label. Or give each child a bag to collect candy scattered around after the birthday piñata's been broken open.

• Use handled, plastic bags to take outgrown children's clothing to the thrift store or charity of your choice.

I also use the self-closing bags for Barbie doll clothes and accessories. My twin girls have so many Barbie doll clothes, doll shoes, doll hangers and all of the very little stuff that comes with Barbie. Those of you who have Barbies around your house know exactly what I mean. What a mess!!! I put everything in self-closing bags, then throw all of the bags into a container. I don't have to worry about vacuuming up any of those little pieces.

Kim Ragle, San Jose, CA

Keep 'em Neat and Clean

• Make a floor cover to put under a highchair or young child's chair by splitting the seams of a large plastic bag. Take one along when you go visiting with small children, too.

• Let small children look at photographs kept in bags to keep photos from being crushed or smudged by overeager little fin-gers. (Plastic bags also work well for storing photos that don't fit in albums.)

• Make disposable aprons
and bibs for young (or old)
out of handled, plastic
T-bags. Cut off the bottom of
the bag so it is open, then up
one side (which becomes the
back) but not into the
handled area, as the handles
become the armholes. Or,
make a quick baby bib in the
same way, using the new
handled, plastic lunch bags.

• Use a plastic bag as a liner under sheets to protect the mattress
of a child not yet dry at night. Take one with you when visiting
others, too.

• Protect your sinks from messes. Keep a few clean, wet paper
towels in a self-closing bag by each sink, so kids can clean themselves up without having to turn on the faucet.

---

*I recently had an ultra sound done. I put it in a self-closing bag
for all to see and to keep it nice.*

Cathy Young, Guthrie, OK

Out and About

• Use a large bag as a suitcase when sleeping over at a friend's,
and carry a sleeping bag in a large, plastic garbage bag.

• Pack a change of clothes for children in a plastic bag that you
keep in your car's trunk in case of any kind of kid-related acci-
dent. Then put the soiled clothes in the bag and secure it closed

till you get home. Consider sending resealable bags to daycare with your children, so the teacher can do the same.

- Put appropriate-size plastic bags (even bread/newspaper bags) over a child's feet before slipping on snow boots. The boots come off without a struggle and feet stay much dryer.

- Use a large, zip-top bag filled about one-third full with baby powder and let kids put their hands and feet in the bag when leaving the beach and before getting into the car. The sand will be removed as they brush off the powder.

- Take an ice-filled, resealable bag to your child's team sports events on hot days. It will feel great on the back of your neck on a really hot day. And if one of the young players gets a bruise or twists an ankle, you can be ready with an ice bag.

- Pack a clean pair of socks in your child's school backpack during the winter months. Socks often get wet, even under boots.

- Keep a few crayons (and maybe some paper) in a resealable bag, in car, purse or pocket, to give kids something to do while waiting for food in a slow-serving restaurant.

- Put snacks in a resealable bag to take to the grocery store for toddlers or young children to keep them occupied and lessen the need for those (usually non-nutritious and expensive) impulse buys.

My daughter packed each day's clothes in a separate gallon-size bag for a Girl Scout camping trip. (It eliminates searching through the bag each morning.) You can use a permanent marker and label the bag with the day it was intended for.
Deborah J. Martin , La Porte, TX

Taking It With You

• Pack all or parts of kids' lunches in resealable bags. They can use the bags to bring home leftovers and there will be no messy "yuck" to clean out of the bottom of the lunch box. Or just use (and reuse several times) a large slider-closing bag as the lunch bag/box itself.

• Put powdered drink mixes in resealable bags to send to school with children. After school, they can combine the drink mix with water in a water bottle, and they won't need to buy a drink from a machine.

• Let an older student keep a bag in his or her briefcase or book bag, filled with the essentials: tape, small stapler, correction fluid, self-stick notes and such.

•Or punch holes along the bottom side of a resealable freezer bag to hold your children's school items fastened right into the front of a three-ring binder. You may want to reinforce the punched edge with duct tape.

• Close up in a plastic bag your business card, a few plastic bandages or any other mini first-aid items and a chocolate kiss (for when Mom or Dad can't be there to kiss it and make it better) and place it in your child's backpack.

• Cover a backpack with a large trash bag to keep it from getting wet. Make slits in the bag to fit the backpack's straps.

• Tuck a plastic newspaper bag in your child's backpack for carrying rolled up art work home from school.

• Have kids carry any needed money to school in a resealable bag labeled with their names.

• Let a child take a toothbrush and toothpaste to school in a resealable bag.

> *My nine-year-old daughter carries her recorder in a slider-closing bag to music classes. That keeps it clean in her backpack and the bag is easy for her to open and close.*
>
> Diane M. O'Neal, Houston, TX

Away From Home

- Hang plastic bags on door knobs in dorm rooms to use as trash bags or gather aluminum cans for recycling.

- Pre-soak dirty laundry in a dorm room. Put the clothes in a bag with a little detergent and water and shake. (Don't leave it too long, however, or the clothes will get moldy.)

- Store and protect fossil and plant specimens for biology classes in resealable plastic bags.

- Put a plastic bag with a pillow or pad in it on a stadium seat when it's raining.

> *I am an avid biology student in college and I have a collection of carnivorous plants. I use the slider-closing bags to store the insects I catch for my plants since the slider locking feature allows me to open and close the bag fast enough to not let anything escape and assures me that the bag is closed (I don't want dinner escaping!)*
>
> Christopher A. Turbeville, Mountain View, CA
>
> *When I took the Arizona Bar, you were not allowed to carry a purse—everything had to fit into a clear plastic bag. As I needed to carry an ID and wallet, I didn't want to lose anything and that was my 'special' use.*
>
> Jan C. Bishop, Cary, IL

Teachers' Uses

• Send books home with children in resealable bags, especially those that are soft bound or in short supply. Students can also take flash cards or school papers home in plastic bags.

• Encourage kids to use resealable bags, instead of a manila folder, for safely keeping materials for class projects. Some teachers use plastic bags to separate math manipulatives and have them ready to be passed out to students.

• Store book sets with related lesson plans in self-closing bags for easier teacher access in media centers.

• Transport students' papers to be graded and returned to students in plastic bags—a good way to keep papers together, yet with names and projects visible.

• Ask students, at the beginning of the year, to bring in extra resealable bags to keep in their desks for the multitude of possible uses.

• Use wet paper towels, stored in a resealable bag, to erase and wash a chalk board.

> *As a speech pathologist who works in a school, I find I can safely store items that need to be kept clean, such as rubber gloves and tongue depressors, in resealable bags.*
> *Karen Louick, Brooklyn, NY*

Projects and Experiments

• Fill resealable bags with a variety of ingredients to make inexpensive and educational toys/games for kids from pre-school through elementary grades. Partly fill a bag with whatever ingredients you're using, squeeze most of the air out, close the bag and lay it flat, smoothing out the ingredients till they're spread evenly. If you want to reinforce the bag, slip another one over it and close that one, too. Then, tape the top shut with duct tape. *(An adult should always supervise this activity.)*

Ingredients you can use:
- to clear or colored hair gel, or hand sanitizer, add tempera paint and/or glitter, small plastic or metallic confetti-type shapes. (Buy these at stationery or greeting card stores.) Put the bag on a table and let pre-school kids squis h the gel and shapes around. They love the texture and feel. For a different "feel," refrigerate the bag first—especially nice on a hot day.
- shaving cream and food coloring or pudding create 'magic slates' for children to practice writing letters, spelling or math facts.
- cooked cornstar ch and water with added food coloring or tempera paint as a 'magic slate.'
- a few tablespoons of ketchup, mustar d—or both— for a squishy painting bag. Kids can draw over the bag with their fingers to create paintings. Erase drawings by smoothing over the bag with the palm of your hand.

- Package individual project kits for technology education classes in resealable bags. Ask students to return the bags after using, then recycle them for the next semester.

- Store samples of powders for chemistry classes, such as sulfur or activated charcoal, in resealable bags. They're easy to transport, there's less chance of spilling and they won't break. Store lab sets for students in the same way. (*WARNING*: Most chemicals should not, however, be stored in plastic bags.)

- Collect, store and transport fossils, plant specimens and other science materials in bags.

> *My daughter had to do a model of a cell. We filled a resealable bag with hair gel and floated stuff in it to resemble a nucleus.*
> Ms. Susan L. Hengel, Wilmington, DE

Arts and Crafts

- Make a traditional kite for a child from six pieces of wood in a kite frame pattern. Cut out a shape to fit the frame from a heavy-duty plastic bag. Secure the plastic to the frame with tape or staples. Add a tail and attach needed string for flying this kite.

- Make a little book for a young child by sewing sandwich-size resealable bags together along the bottom edge, either by hand or machine. (An overcast stitch works fine.) Cut thin cardboard to fit inside the bags and use both sides of each bag. Change the pictures in this book to keep it interesting. For an older child, use a larger bag and put together books on different "subjects," for example, a book on dogs, one on babies, and the like. Or use to hold flash cards and math tables.

- Put together a collage bag containing newspaper and magazine clippings, children's scissors and paste and let kids make their own work of art on a rainy day when there's nothing to do.

- Make edible play-dough for kids in a resealable pint-size plastic bag. Combine: 1 part creamy, shelf-stable peanut butter and 2 parts dry ingredients such as flour, toasted wheat germ, chocolate drink mix or blenderized uncooked oatmeal. Kids can mix the ingredients themselves in the closed bag without getting their hands messy. Chill in the refrigerator so it is less sticky. Add more dry ingredients if necessary.

- Make and store your own homemade play-dough. In a large, resealable bag combine 1-1/2 cups flour, a few drops of oil and colored water (use a bit of food coloring) a little at a time until mixture is consistency of bread dough. Close the bag and knead ingredients well. Stored in the refrigerator, it will keep moist and fresh for a long time. Separate the dough into small, plastic snack bags to use or give as gifts or party favors.

• Store paints and paint brushes in separate bags for future use.

• Color macaroni for crafts projects by putting the macaroni, a bit of rubbing alcohol and food coloring in a zipped bag and shaking it all up. Instant colored macaroni with no mess!

• Manage glitter projects by first putting glue in one bag and cutting a small corner off (this is easier for children to use than a glue bottle) and, second, putting glitter in another bag, in which you've made holes with fork tines (more or fewer holes, depending on the child's age).

Kid Fun

• For baby play, put into a sturdy plastic shopping bag lots of different objects with interesting shapes: a large plastic kitchen spoon with holes in it, a large key ring with plastic objects attached, plastic measuring spoons linked with a ring, small plastic bowl, a small doll, and the like. Put two or three different objects inside the bag each day and place it in front of the child on the floor. Show the child what is inside. Watch what he or she does. *(Make sure all objects are too large for the child to choke on.)*

• Fill a bag with water, place metallic confetti inside and zip the bag closed. It's a great water-filled outdoor or pool toy.

• Have "Movie Night" for the kids. Make popcorn and put into individual resealable bags, one for each child. *(WARNING: Popcorn is considered a choking hazard for children under age 3.)*

• Make a jump rope from bread bags. Split the bags down the side seams to make long pieces of plastic. Braid three lengths together. When you get to the end of the piece, wrap another bag end around the first. Stagger joinings to prevent a clump. Create handles out of duct tape.

Family Time and Traditions

My grandson, who is 2, has to have his "own" bag of Cheerios, cookies, etc. Every time he visits, he goes right to the drawer and grabs a self-closing bag and hands it to me to fill. He loves opening and closing the bag! It's better than toys to him!
                                                    Jan Mohondro, Walpole, MA

My mother keeps change in slide locking bags in the kitchen to have on hand to give the younger grandkids quarters.
                                        Stephanie Stoltman, Minnstonka, MN

When each of our children was born, I saved a copy of the newspaper of that day in an airtight resealable bag. I plan on giving it to them on their 21st birthday.
                                        Stephen A. Wowelko, East Syracuse, NY

A resealable bag is a great way to keep the lock of hair from my little girl's first haircut as a memento.
                                        Mrs. Jeff L. Hartzheim, Jefferson, LA

I have each of my children's dried umbilical cords in them. It sounds gross, I know, but I'm sure plenty of other moms save them, too.
                                        Maura Philipps, Staten Island, NY

PAPER CHASE AND OTHER PARAPHERNALIA

The Business of Life
• Organize and neatly store sales receipts, warranties, parts lists and booklets that come with appliances. Punch holes in self-closing bags to fit a three-ring binder, then slip all information

about each appliance into a separate bag and seal. Consider saving important papers such as insurance, titles or birth certificates the same way.

• Keep a large ball of twine neatly inside a self-closing storage bag. Punch a small hole in the side so twine can be pulled out without unwinding the entire ball. Store it in a drawer.

• Save offer forms and UPC codes for rebates in resealable bags and file them in a small box until all needed items are collected.

• Or save all coupons and proof-of-purchases, by category, in separate plastic bags.

• Collect small items such as broken jewelry, batteries to be replaced or screws to be used for repairs in resealable bags until you can deal with them.

• Keep items you buy in large packages (cotton swabs, cotton balls, wet wipes) clean and organized by storing in smaller resealable bags.

I put all my receipts for tax time in resealable bags. I then put the year on the outside of the bag. This keeps everything for the year together and is very easy to open up and look for something when I need to. I save my receipts from other years, too. It is very easy to put many bags in the same box. Nothing gets mixed up. It works great!

Sharon A. Wirth, Milwaukee, WI

Our business serves legal papers to people. Under certain circumstances, we have to leave the papers on a door latch or door knob. When that is necessary, we use a self-closing bag to keep the papers dry and intact.

Anonymous

Mail Call

- Use a gallon-size resealable bag to hold all the things you need for correspondence and bills, from stationery and pens to stamps and return address stickers, so you don't have to spend time collecting all these items when you're ready to sit down and pay bills or drop a note to someone.

- Protect videocassettes you send through the mail by putting them first in an air-inflated, self-closing bag. Try this also for any small or breakable items, or even homemade greeting cards, that need protection while going through the mail.

- Keep some bags near the place where you open your mail and put into them any small samples you receive that you'll use for travel. When a bag is full, put it in your suitcase, so you're ready for a trip.

- Seal leakable items, if you're mailing them in a package, in resealable bags in case they happen to break during shipping.

- Zip outgoing mail into a bag to protect it from the elements until it's picked up, in case the mailbox leaks.

I keep different denominations of stamps separated in my desk drawer using small plastic bags.
                                        Marty Rauch, Los Angeles, CA

I'm a letter carrier and I keep a resealable bag in my mail bag with dog treats for all the nasty doggies out there.
                                        Lori K. Oneil, Englewood, CO

When I was in the Peace Corps, I kept important papers in a resealable bag. This kept things like letters from home and my bank book from getting soaked by rain or by being in proximity to other wet things.
                                        Bart Briefstein, Great Neck, NY

Keepsakes and Photos

- Place negatives in a plastic zip-top snack bag, labeled with date and description, and they'll be protected and easy to find when you want them.

- Keep birth and wedding announcements or other special newspaper clippings accessible and in good condition in resealable plastic bags.

- Bury your time capsule contents in a resealable freezer bag to protect them.

Work/Office

- Keep pens, pencils and small office supplies separated in plastic bags in your briefcase.

- Protect computer disks from dust and moisture damage by storing them in self-closing plastic bags.

- Store computer cables, circuit boards and power adapters in plastic bags, too. And put cords and accessories from a laptop computer into separate, labeled bags before packing them in your carrying case.

- Use plastic bags to store inkjet cartridges to keep them from drying out. Transport the cartridges with minimal mess by packing them in self-closing bags, too.

- Keep a self-closing bag handy, if you work in an office, to collect the small paper circles from a three-hole punch. Save the circles to use as confetti for weddings or other celebrations.

- Drop cash deposits in the safe or at the bank in slide locking bags. They are reusable but still expendable.

- If you work in a retail store, consider bagging up anti-theft sensors, hanger clips and other small objects that accumulate.

I am in charge of several publicity events. I have lots of items that I have to transport from my office to the event venue. I use self-closing bags to keep items such as press passes, pencils, buttons and badges organized by type.
                                        Phoebe Resnick, Wallingford, PA

I work in a prison hospital and our belongings are searched every day when we enter work. I put my things in a self-closing bag so the staff can see them without opening the bag. It saves time for both of us.
                                        Josette L. Rowe, Brooklyn, MI

Unaccustomed as I am to Public Speaking...

• Use small bags to store index cue cards for speeches.

Many times I have to leave a note for someone outside on my front door or, as a realtor, I have to leave instructions for people, so I write the note and enclose it in a self-closing bag and tack it up where all can see. With the winter upon us, I'm able to leave the notes out in the most horrible weather and they stay dry and, most important, I'm assured they can be read!
                                        Sally Brush, Cincinnati, OH

HEALTH CONCERNS

Kit & Kaboodle

• Fill a few zip-top plastic bags with a mixture of half-water and half-alcohol. These will not freeze solid, so they make good moldable compresses for bumps, bruises, toothaches or puffy eyes. And they can be refrozen and used again. (If you're going to use one for more than a few minutes, wrap the bag in a napkin, washcloth or towel to protect your skin.)

Other suggestions for bag "fillers" to be kept in freezer:
- ice cubes (5 -6 cubes, 1/4 cup water and a little salt)
- crushed ice
- wet sponge or washcloth
- frozen vegetables (especially peas, as an alternative to gel eye masks)
- unpopped popcorn
- rolled up baby washcloths (for babies' teething pain)

I recently had surgery for knee replacement and needed an ice bag. None could be found that were large enough. I took the larger bag, filled it 3/4 full of water and added rubbing alcohol and put it in the freezer. The rubbing alcohol keeps it at a nice mushy freeze and can be used day after day. I used mine every day for several months during therapy and the bags do not leak.
Maxine H. Frank, Windom, MN

- Use a damp, warm washcloth in a plastic bag as a compress, when heat is called for. Or make a heating pad by putting a wet cloth in a resealable bag and microwaving on High for 30 seconds. You can reheat it whenever you need to. It's easier than a hot water bottle and more portable than an electric heating pad.

- Or heat for one minute, 2 cups oatmeal and 1 cup water shaken up in a bag. Soothing for arthritis pain.

- Portion out daily amounts of food for special diets and keep them in resealable bags. And, keep cut up fruits and vegetables handy in plastic bags, too, for those "snack attacks."

- Carry medicines that need to be kept cold in a resealable bag with ice (if casing is water-tight) or insert a frozen gel-pac.

- Make a mini-first aid kit with things like aspirin, antiseptic ointment, adhesive bandages and alcohol pads in a resealable bag and keep it handy at home or in the car.

Personal Hygiene

- Clean dentures overnight in a resealable bag with cleaner.

- Use a zip-top bag, in place of its case, to hold a retainer. Easy for a teen to slip a bag in a pocket.

- Have the men in your family keep all their shaving supplies in their own resealable bags. It keeps the bathroom organized and the countertop clean.

- Use a self-closing bag to carry vitamins or any ointments that have a pretty foul smell.

I work for a private ambulance service. Many of our calls require us to start an IV and sometimes we really have to get it done fast. There are many small pieces of equipment we need and they easily get lost in our jump kits. We use self-closing bags to store packages with gauze, capped IV catheters, alcohol wipes and opti-sites (they cover the IV site.) We package each little kit in its own bag and don't have to struggle to find all our equipment when we really need it. These bags come in handy when a life is on the line!

Stacie M. Hansen, Valley City, ND

...And Beauty

- Keep the cosmetics you use every morning in a resealable bag and everything will be in one place, visible and easy to find.

- Store hair supplies such as ribbons, barrettes, pony tail holders, curlers and scrunchies in plastic bags. You can even color coordinate them. Also, store a haircutting kit, if you do the family's haircuts.

- Soften your hands by covering them with petroleum jelly and slipping them into plastic storage bags. Wait 15 minutes, then wash hands with warm water.

- Blow up a large plastic bagwith air and seal it shut to use as a pillow when soaking in a bathtub or hot tub.

- And if a lost drain plug is keeping you from that needed soak, fill a sandwich bag with water. Leaving it open, place it filled in the drain hole then run your bath. The bag will keep the water from draining out until you are ready to remove it.

In Sickness...and in Health

- Cut apples, carrots, celery and oranges into small pieces and put them in resealable bags. They will be handy to munch on whenever a nicotine or diet-related craving hits.

- Use a large-size plastic bag to keep a cast on a broken leg or arm dry while showering.

- Keep a large, resealable bag handy to hold used tissues when family members have a cold or flu. It's easy to keep germs contained and the whole lot can be disposed of when the bag is full.

- Cope with motion sickness by keeping a few cotton balls in a resealable bag with a drop or two of lavender oil. When feeling queasy, open the bag and inhale for a minute or two.

- Use a large, zip-top bag to line a plastic bowl or trash basket for anyone who is throwing up at home or in the car, to minimize the odor.

- Are your spending habits becoming bad for your health? Fill a self-closing bag with water, add credit cards and freeze, if you have a problem with compulsive overspending. You'll have time to think while waiting for the bag to defrost.

FOR ANIMAL LOVERS

Smart Pet Tricks

- Slide a large, plastic grocery bag over one end of a cat litter box, hold it by the handles and tip up the opposite end, spilling the litter into the bag. Or use one to line the litter box—less expensive than the commercial liners.

- Recycle long, plastic newspaper or bread bags as pooper-scoopers. Put the bag on like a glove, scoop the poop, then turn it inside out, tie the top in a knot and dispose of it.

- Or use a zip-top bag, seal and dispose of, to avoid odor.

- Or use a "needs-to-be-recycled" bag when sifting out clumping cat litter. Also, store your cat's pooper scooper in its own resealable bag.

- Make a temporary cat toy by blowing up, then closing, a small freezer-weight resealable bag. It will last longer than a balloon.

When someone's dog poops on my lawn, I go outside, hand them a plastic bag and say, 'Oh, I think you must've forgotten this.' (I guess I win the prize for diplomacy.)
                                                        Pat Taylor, Rochester, MN

We have a dog who loves restaurant leftovers. It has become my habit to always carry a self-closing bag in my handbag because "doggy bags" are not always available and wrapping messy food in a napkin can ruin the lining of a nice purse. Self-closing bags are light, take up no room and can safely carry home even the remains of a Caesar Salad, which happens to be Salty's favorite dish.

                                                        Suzi Resnik, Del Mar, CA

Pet Corner

- Use a large, resealable bag to store an opened bag of dry pet food to keep it fresh and free of infestations.

- Or seal an opened can of pet food in a zip-top bag to keep odors from permeating throughout the rest of the fridge.

- Store catnip in a resealable bag, so it doesn't lose its potency.

- Store in a plastic bag the frozen brine shrimp that you use to feed fish in your fish tank.

- Accustom a fish that you've bought at a pet store to your at-home aquarium by floating it in a resealable, water-filled bag in the tank for about an hour, so it won't be shocked by different water temperatures.

- Or use resealable bags anytime you have to move or clean the aquarium. Use the sturdiest bags, as flimsy ones can be poked through by sharp fish fins.

- Use plastic bags in the horse stable or when traveling to shows to keep supplies such as brushes, powders, shampoos and hoof polish and the first aid kit clean and organized.

- Keep treats for dogs in resealable bags as rewards for good behavior when training or traveling. Also, when traveling with pets, carry their toys in a resealable bag.

- Store odor-laden cat treats in plastic bags for a cat who hates to travel in the car.

> *We also use self-sealing bags outdoors to bring water for our dog and we have her trained so that when we open the bag, she sticks her head in and drinks. An instant water bowl for the pet on the move!*
>
> *Valerie L. Evans, San Jose, CA*

For the Birds...and Other Outdoor Animals

- Store birdseed in large, resealable bags. Put out as much as space will allow and keep the rest fresh till you need it.

- Or mix birdseed with peanut butter inside a self-closing bag to keep your hands clean. Transfer to a small net bag and hang outside for birds.

- Fill bags with acorns in the fall. Then, when it's cold and wintry, let the kids take them out to feed your squirrels.

> *When we have to leave our dog at the babysitter's (yes, our hound has a babysitter!) we always measure out her food into self-closing bags. That way, there's no fussing with putting her meal together.*
> *Diane M. Costello, Ellicott City, MD*

CRAFTS & HOBBIES

Craft Creativity

- When working with two or more balls of yarn or thread, put the balls in a plastic bag and make small holes in the bag to thread each yarn through. The balls will stay clean and untangled. Or, put a ball of yarn in a plastic bag and feed the yarn through a hole in the bottom of the bag. The yarn will feed out as you use it, but will not unwind or tangle. Or have the yarn coming out the space after closing the zipper top almost to the end.

- Slide small paint palettes into resealable bags to preserve the paints for the next time you want to use them.

- Store leftover colored sand for constructing sand creations in separate plastic bags.

- Stuff throw pillows with excess plastic bags and they'll be soft and full. Remove bags before washing pillow covers.

- Save broken crayons, stored in resealable bags, and melt them down for candle-making. Do the same with candle stubs.

- Shake craft items that need stiffening in a resealable bag with liquid starch. Any leftover starch can remain in the zipped-up bag for next time.

Sew or knit two pieces of fabric together to form a purse. Place a slide locking bag snugly in between and sew up the bottom. You now have the perfect travel bag to carry make-up or toothbrushes! I prefer black velvet fabric. It adds an elegant touch, and I've even taken my slide locking purse along with me to dinner parties.
Cheryl M. Sarges, Woodbury, MN

I have found that the easiest way to dry flowers is to fill a self-closing bag three-quarters full with silicon gel and add flowers. Close up bag and gently shake. Leave for several days to a week.
Barbara M. Jones, Rutherfordton, NC

Keepin' it Together

- Organize quilting scraps, threads for cross-stitch, needlepoint or machine sewing, yarn for knitting or hooking rugs and store them all in separate bags. Store sewing patterns in bags, too, with the original envelope in front to identify pattern.

- Separate and bag all the small sewing supplies that get mixed together and/or lost in the bottom of your sewing basket.

- Store any and all crafts projects, especially tiny items such as beads and sequins, in plastic bags. You won't lose small parts or pieces.

- Keep computer disks containing designs created for a particular craft project in a self-closing bag stapled to the inside of your craft instruction book.

- Dye macaroni by putting the macaroni, rubbing alcohol and food coloring in a resealable bag and shaking. Colored macaroni in an instant!

One of my hobbies is making very delicate (museum quality) feather ornaments and, when I cut and sort feathers, some are quite small and might easily be lost, so I use self-closing bags to store the many different sizes. At a glance, I can see the many sizes and colors, and the bags prevent the feathers from flying off the table in the event that I forget and breathe too heavily.
Adrian Vaughan, Hillsborough, NC

I am constantly working on plastic canvas projects that involve lots of small pieces as well as many different colors of yarn. I use resealable bags to keep the pieces organized and I save each color yarn in a separate bag. The bags are easy to label and keep my supplies nice and neat!
Debbie G. Majury , Bloomingdale, NJ

...And Clean

- Cover flowers that you're drying for decorative purposes with plastic bags punched with air holes, so they'll stay dust-free.

- Keep clay, paints, markers and other art materials fresh and reusable by storing them in a zip-top bag. Put your whole painting palette or plate with various oil or acrylic paints into a large bag between painting sessions.

Hobby Helpers

- Store such collectibles as sports cards and comics in resealable plastic bags.

- Keep Beanie Babies clean and organized in individual bags.

- Store each classic 45 RPM record in a separate bag to keep it in good condition.

- Carry shooter marbles to and from the circular arena in resealable bags.

- Carry extra dart tips and flights in self-closing bags.

- Keep small car parts together if you take apart and restore old cars, so you can categorize the parts and nothing gets lost. Also, use bags to protect hands when cleaning and polishing the car or changing oil and other fluids.

- Take treated rags to antique car shows in separate, resealable bags for wiping down, drying and dusting cars. Rags with vinyl cleaner can be kept separate from those with a protectant or tire cleaner.

I use them in my antiques and collectibles business. I ship many things all over the U.S. When there is a delicate item that would be damaged if any moisture got to it, I put it in a resealable bag. I then inflate the bag, so not only does the bag protect it from moisture, but also cushions it along the way.
Melanie A. Mason, Arlington, TX

I use resealable bags to store photographic film. They protect my film while it's being stored in the refrigerator or freezer. I make sure the film warms to room temperature before I open the bag to prevent moisture from condensing on it.
Gail E. Phillips, Berkeley, CA

Leisure Activities

- Love movies, but hate to pay the prices for snacks? Sneak popcorn or other snacks into the movies (if you have a big enough purse) in resealable bags, of course.

- Put your journal in a resealable bag, along with pen or pencil, to keep everything handy, clean and portable.

- Store a deck of playing cards in a resealable bag. It will outlast the paper box it came in.

- Use bags to hold Bingo supplies. Keep the same amount of Bingo chips in each bag, so the chips don't have to be counted again each time they're used.

- Keep computer game accessories clean and dust-free in resealable bags.

> *I used a resealable bag to put my Scrabble game tiles in! It works just great.*
> *Roseanne M. Lewis-Maloney, Cleveland, OH*
>
> *As an occasional visitor to the casinos in Las Vegas, I prefer to use plastic bags rather than those plastic cups the casinos provide.*
> *Winnie Kuzara, Minnetonka, MN*

TRAVEL

Going Places

- When traveling by car with small children, line the bottom of a travel potty with a small, plastic garbage bag and place a disposable diaper in the bottom to prevent sloshing. Dispose of when convenient.

- Keep some plastic handled bags in the car. They'll come in handy for lots of things: a quickie baby bib; litter bag; car snacks; carrying kids' small toys and crayons...or for those unfortunate instances of motion sickness.

- Take a gallon-size bag along to make a blow-up pillow to use for naps in the car, at the beach or camping.

- Bringing back a delicate item? Wrap it well, place it in a sturdy plastic bag, blow air into the bag and tie it shut. This will give you an extra cushion of protection.

- Use plastic bags to carry damp clothes home after a trip, picnic or day at the beach. Also, put damp workout clothing or bathing suits in plastic bags to keep everything else in your gym bag dry and fresh-smelling. Carry after-shower supplies in a resealable bag, too.

- Pack snacks for a car trip in resealable plastic bags. For children, pack in snack-size bags. Let kids keep the bags with them and try to make the snacks last throughout the day's trip.

- Keep a wet washcloth in a self-closing bag to wipe the driver's face to keep him or her alert.

- Carry a box of resealable bags in the car for those times when you spot wild berries or mushrooms and stop to pick them.

For long trips, I pack plastic forks and knives in the bags. As the forks and knives diminish, the bags become useful for the tiny/ large memories that my child wants to bring back to share with the class.

Rita K. Fleischmann, Columbia, MO

A group of us visited Israel and one brave soul used a slide-locking bag to bring back mud from the Dead Sea.

Karen Klempel, San Diego, CA

While You're Away...

• Care for plants while you're gone with either of these two
  methods:

  ¤ Group your well-watered plants on a tray of wet gravel
    and cover with a large, transparent plastic bag. Put the
    plants in a cool place out of bright or direct sunlight.

  ¤ Or, line the bathtub with plastic bags and cover the bags
    with a wet beach towel. Set plants on the towel and water
    them one last time.

Packing Pointers

• Slip extra luggage keys in a small bag and carry in purse or
  pocket in case you misplace your first set.

• Use resealable bags to pack and separate small travel items,
  such as cotton balls and swabs, safety pins, nail polish, contact
  lens kit and any leakable toilet articles. Use large bags for various clothing items.

• Place your hanging clothes in dry cleaning bags before putting
  them into a garment bag or suitcase and they'll arrive with fewer
  wrinkles.

• Pack like items (such as underwear or socks) in large plastic
  bags. You can unpack in just a few moves and your clothes stay
  organized. Put all your shoes in plastic bags, to protect your
  clothing.

• Pack a change of underwear and necessary toilet articles in a
  resealable bag to carry with you on a plane. If your luggage is
  lost, you'll have what you need for at least the next day.

• Pack a large trash bag or two in your luggage. It's perfect for
  toting back dirty laundry and a black one makes an excellent
  emergency raincoat or wind breaker under your coat—just cut
  slits for head and arms.

- Use a small, resealable bag to act as your traveling soap "dish." Or bring one along to hold and take home the hotel soap bar you do use.

> *When on a trip and you want to pack dirty clothes and keep them separate from your clean ones, put into a self-closing bag. Close bag about three-quarters of the way. Roll bag to squeeze out all of the air. Fasten the rest of the way while still rolled. Keeps the dirt and odor away from your other clothes, yet takes less room than your clothes normally take.*
>
> > *H. Louise Mitchell, Campbell, CA*
>
> *My son is in the Marines. When we picked him up from Boot Camp he had EVERYTHING in resealable bags, from his writing supplies to his orders! He said it was the best way to stay organized while living out of a foot locker!!*
>
> > *Marla A. Brugger, Shamokin , PA*

Packing Kids' Stuff

- Pack one day's clothes (matching top and bottom, underwear and socks) in a self-closing plastic bag when traveling. Reuse the bag at night for soiled clothes.

- Let kids pack their own Travel (plastic) Bag, with favorite small toys, crayons, coloring books and games or books-on-tape.

- Zip up a set of Books-on-Tape with a Walkman and a spare set of batteries to occupy kids (or anyone!) on a long trip.

The 'Bayer' Necessities

- Pack an "Emergency Kit," which might include bandages, aspirin, antiseptic ointment, safety pins and trial-size packages of powdered detergent.

- Keep medications/vitamins in one handy bag or, if you take lots of different ones, separate them into several smaller bags.

- Enclose ear plugs in small, resealable bags.

- Pre-moisten cotton balls with insect repellent to carry with you in a small bag.

> *Plastic bags are great for carrying false teeth.*
>   *Mrs. Ted Federoff, Elyria, OH*

Other Travel Tips

- Store your passport, binoculars, camera , film and maps in a resealable bag to keep them water- and dirt-proof.

- Use plastic bags for getting film and computer disks through airport checkpoints without their having to undergo x-ray. Security guards can see through the bag.

- When you're traveling and have to take your own washcloth and towel, put damp towels and washcloths in bags and close up in the morning. Other packed things stay dry and you can air out the towels at the end of the day.

- Keep souvenirs fresh and in one place to take home and put in your scrapbook or preserve in whatever way you choose. Or, once you're home, you can organize them in the same bags.

- Pack some coffee filters in a bag to take to a timeshare condo or any short-term vacation rental. They often will supply a coffee maker, but not always enough filters.

> *I use it to carry sand in whenever I travel and am near a beach. I collect the sand and some shells and put it into a self-closing bag and mark the area and date on it. Crazy collection, but fond memories.*
>   *Frances M. Gazvoda, Cleveland, OH*

On Your Purse(on)

- Fill a bag with packets of instant coffee, creamer and sweetener to carry in your purse for a quick cup when you need it.

- Carry bottled water in a resealable bag in case the bottle leaks.

- Keep a resealable bag in your purse for restaurant leftovers (and they don't have to be for the dog). Plastic bags are more convenient than the styrofoam containers and, when zipped closed, won't leak or allow food to go stale.

- Make up your own small packs of tissues in plastic sandwich bags. They're less expensive than the ones you buy prepackaged.

- Use a small, plastic bag for a sewing kit with needles threaded with different colors of thread, a thimble, a few buttons and a small scissors. Keep one in your purse, car or desk at work.

- Carry some toilet paper in a self-closing bag and keep in your purse at all times in case of emergency. Actually, packing a roll that is almost finished in a bag is one way to keep the bag small and manageable.

- Use different, resealable snack-size or pint-size bags to hold foreign money when traveling abroad—one for each country!

- Carry a bag with ice cubes in it if you have to wait for a bus in very hot weather and apply to face and neck to keep from getting overheated. Pop an ice cube into your mouth to keep cool.

- Keep a small sandwich bag in your purse to collect trash trivia you can then throw away easily.

- Fold a medium-size plastic bag until it is the size of a package of gum. Secure it with a rubber band and drop into the bottom of your purse. You'll be surprised how often it comes in handy.

On "Auto"-matic

- Keep car interiors smelling fresh. Fill a bag with potpourri and open it as needed.

- Use a small plastic bag to keep change for tolls handy in one place.

- Store auto registration, proof of insurance and any other pertinent papers in a resealable bag in the glove compartment.

- Or for maintaining travel expense receipts and turnpike and toll expense records.

- Keep one (or more) large trash bags in your car's glove compartment or trunk for an emergency "raincoat." Just make a slit for head and arms and you're set.

I find resealable bags great for storing topographic maps. The maps can be refolded to allow your current location to be visible through the bag so the map does not have to be exposed to the elements.
Gary V. Wolff, Wichita, KS

Vehicle Breakdowns

- Carry wet, soapy rags and dry towels for clean-up, if you're handy enough to take care of automotive problems yourself.

- Keep plastic bags in the car toolbox to safely hold small parts you remove when you change a tire or make another roadside repair.

- Use a zip-top bag to hold one or more emergency flares in the trunk, even homemade ones, such as empty milk cartons stuffed with newspaper.

Car Talk

• If your car isn't kept in a garage overnight in cold weather, cover your side mirror with a plastic bag, held in place with a clothespin (or, if it's a resealable bag, zip it up) and the mirror will be clear in the morning.

• Place a cut-open plastic shopping bag under the windshield wipers (after first setting the wipers in straight up position) to keep car windshields free of ice and snow. The bag will adhere to the window and you can peel it off when you're ready to go.

• Keep a few bread or newspaper bags in your glove compartment to protect hands when pumping gas.

• Use an empty tissue box to hold some of the many excess plastic bags that come into your home. Keep them in your car for a variety of uses. The box is a good, compact container for bags of all sizes that won't take up much space wherever you use it.

• Store your car's registration and insurance information in a resealable bag in your glove compartment. They'll be protected and easy to find, too.

• Use small, plastic bags for litter in your car. Handled bags can easily "hang" from your dashboard.

• Slip plastic trash bags on the garage floor under the car to catch those last few drops of oil after an oil change.

> *When I change my car's oil and filter, I put the used oil filter inside a resealable bag and just toss it into the trash. It saves mess and time.*
>
> *Nancy L Ziembo, Saginaw, MI*

THE GREAT OUT-OF-DOORS

Winter
• Keep ski lift tickets dry and readable in a resealable bag.

• Use a large trash bag tied around you diaper-fashion for an impromptu sled.

• Keep all your "carry-ons" dry and easy-to-find while snowmobiling by storing them in resealable plastic bags.

Fishing
• Use resealable bags to store fishing bait. Artificial worms won't dry out and change color and real worms will live if stored with a little damp earth. Put the bag in a cooler on a hot day.

• Place a half-dozen minnows in a resealable bag, seal and store in your pocket when moving along a stream or riverbank. It's easier than carrying a minnow bucket.

• Store fly-tying feathers and other related items in plastic bags.

• Put a damp washcloth in a plastic bag with two or three slices of lemon to freshen your hands after baiting a hook.

• Bring bags filled with seasonings, fillet your catch next to the river or lake and store your fish in plastic bags in the ice chest till you return home or to camp. Fish will be marinated, ready to cook, fresh and tasty.

• Fill a resealable bag with your fish and water, squeeze air out and freeze. Stored this way, fish don't develop freezer burn. (You can store smoked fish in bags in the freezer, too.)

• Don't worry about bringing your cell phone with you. It will stay dry if you keep it in a resealable bag.

> *I put bait in self-closing bags, freeze, take out of freezer, thaw, go fishing and reseal and refreeze over and over.*
>
> *J.R. Brown, Jacksonville, NC*

And Other Water Sports

• Keep small items dry in a scuba diving emergency kit you put together in a plastic bag.

• Slide wetsuit pants on easily by first covering your foot with a plastic bag, especially if your suit is already wet.

• Store surfboard wax in a resealable bag.

• Keep keys dry in a plastic zip-top bag in your wetsuit when surfing. At the beach or a pool, put valuables in a bag in a swimsuit pocket that closes up.

• Keep dampness out of dry foods on a boat by putting them in resealable bags.

• Store and have easy access to small rigging parts on a sailboat by putting them in plastic bags. Keep maps and boat registration papers in resealable bags taped under the dash or seat.

• Fill a few large, resealable bags with mud or wet sand and tie a rope around them as an anchor for a small boat.

• Put small valuables in a resealable bag that you blow into and inflate when boating. If it accidentally goes overboard, it will stay dry and won't sink immediately, giving you a little extra time to retrieve it.

Golf/Baseball

- Use individual, small resealable bags in your golf bag for gloves, tees, ball markers, change and other golfing paraphernalia.

- Make practice golf balls using excess plastic bags you have around the house. Wad several bags into a golf ball shape and wrap the whole thing with a layer of masking tape. You can use these for driving practice in your back yard. (It's much cheaper than going to the driving range.) These practice balls don't travel too far, but will hook or slice just like a real golf ball, giving you the chance to learn how to avoid those problems.

- Put a washcloth and ice in a resealable bag to apply to your head and neck when you get overheated on a hot day on the golf course.

- Store baseball glove oil in a resealable bag inside your bat bag to have handy when you need it.

Runners Take Note

- Deposit keys and personal belongings in a self-sealing bag when running races. You can pick them up, intact, after the race. For daily runs: keep tissues, ID and insurance (or whatever pertinent things you need to carry with you) in a resealable snack-size bag that can fit in your pocket.

- Put a tee-shirt in a resealable bag if you do Triathlons. After the swim portion, you'll have a dry tee-shirt to put on and your race number will stay dry, too.

Cycling

- Use zip-top bags for anything you want to keep dry (and find easily) while motorcycling or bike touring. Keep the plastic bags inside saddle bags and be aware that even leather saddle bags are not waterproof.

• Put a damp towel with a little soap on it in a resealable bag to clean your helmet after motorcycling.

Sports Support

• Put dry gloves in a plastic bag for the soccer goalie, so he or she can change gloves during a damp game.

• Keep first-aid supplies in a bag for injuries that might occur.

• Carry a mouth guard in a resealable bag for any sport for which you'll need one.

In the Stands

• Take an ice-filled, resealable bag to a summer sports event. It feels great to put on the back of your neck on a really hot day.

• Carry a large, plastic trash bag with you to a sporting event (or concert) and keep your coat clean and out of the way by storing it in the bag under your seat.

For the Hunter

• Carry ammunition for target practice in a zip-top bag.

• Keep powder and shells dry in resealable bags when hunting. Also, store shells of different sizes in separate bags.

• Keep hunting clothes free of household smells by washing them in unscented detergent and storing them in resealable bags until hunting season comes around.

• Keep the odor of hunting scents contained by storing worn clothes in resealable bags.

• Make bow hunting gloves smell like the forest and cover household scents by keeping them in a bag with pine needles.

- When hunting, use resealable bags to keep animal parts, such as deer kidneys, separate and fresh right after dressing.

Water Winners

- Keep chlorine tablets for your pool zipped up in a resealable bag and out of children's reach.

- Place a cordless phone or radio in a resealable bag to take to pool or beach to avoid water damage.

- Put rings and watches in a plastic bag at pool or beach so they don't get lost in the water or sand.

- Keep pool or beach snacks in resealable bags. No dishes to remember or items to break.

- Carry tanning lotion or sunscreen tubes or bottles in their own, individual bags. They'll stay sand-free and won't spill on other things in your beach or pool bag.

- Or eliminate the tubes and bottles altogether. Pre-moisten cotton squares with sunscreen and put them in a resealable bag to take to the beach.

- Do the same with pre-moistened squares of astringent or insect repellent, to take off the sunscreen and refresh yourself after the sun or to keep the bugs from biting you.

- Carry beach toys in a large plastic bag with a few holes punched in it for drainage. You can put sandy toys–right in the bag–in the water to drain clean.

- Take plenty of empty bags with you to the beach for kids' collections of seashore treasures and for wet, sandy swimsuits.

> We also use them to keep money and glasses dry when we go to
> amusement parks that have water rides.
>   Monica McLean, Potomac, MD

Outdoor Life

• Enclose a flashlight in a resealable bag to protect it from rain.
  You can turn it on and off without removing it; the light shines
  through the plastic.

• Keep camera film in a bag in an ice chest or cooler when you're
  outdoors in hot weather.

• Pack women's feminine hygiene products in resealable bags to
  keep them clean and dry wherever you go.

Food for Thought

• Avoid carrying a heavy charcoal bag and keep your car clean
  by transporting charcoal to picnics in a resealable bag. Put the
  charcoal lighter fluid in a bag, too, and make it leak-proof.

• Place the ice for your cooler inside sealed bags and keep food
  and other items dry as well as cool. The ice is contained and,
  once melted, provides clean, cool drinking water.

• Or if you don't need much space and aren't going far from home,
  take along a makeshift cooler—just put drinks and ice in a
  resealable bag.

• Do you camp or picnic regularly? Just reuse those bags in which
  the ice has melted by putting the bags of water back in the freezer
  for next time you need them.

• Bring cut-up meat, marinating in a bag, and store it in a cooler
  until you're ready to cook up kabobs.

• Problems packing pickles for a picnic? Glass jars are heavy and breakable, so put the pickles in a resealable bag with a bit of the pickle juice and zip it closed.

> *Give hikers their own individual bags of trail mix in a resealable bag, or even give them two-one to eat while hiking and one in their backpacks—for available food, in case they get lost.*
> Carol Dickman, Colorado Springs, CO

Camping

• On camping trips, store matches, maps, medications and first-aid supplies, utensils, food and clothes in zip-top bags. Boy Scouts use resealable bags to store dryer lint, which they use for starting campfires.

• Keep your sleeping bag dry on camping trips by lining the ground under it with large trash bags.

• Use a small, resealable bag as a soap holder, for showering or just washing up.

• Measure the amounts of food you need and bring them along in individual resealable bags to save space and the weight of packaging.

• Carry cereal in individual bags, filled half-way. When ready to eat, just add milk, then dispose of the bag, and there is no dish to wash.

• Make scrambled eggs while camping by cracking eggs into the bag, zipping closed and shaking to mix.

• Clean eating utensils on a camping trip by adding them to water and antibacterial dish soap in a resealable bag and shaking.

> *Take some extra bags along for trash that should not be left at campsites, such as old food that animals will get into. They also help block the smell of food from animals.*
> *Tim Lambert, Vail, CO*

Weather Protection

• Line the inside of your backpack or bicycle pack with plastic bags to keep water out. Or just place a plastic bag over the pack when it rains.

• Use a newspaper bag as an umbrella cover on wet days. Tuck the bag in your purse or pocket. When you enter a car or building, pull it out and drop your wet umbrella in it.

HOLIDAY HELPERS

Christmas Decor

• Protect gifts you're bringing with you on holiday trips and visits from rain and snow by putting them in large, plastic bags.

• Seal (as best you can) the connections between strings of out side holiday lights 'inside' a small self-sealing bag to keep out moisture and eliminate the chance of electrical problems.

• Prevent a "needle trail" when you take down your Christmas tree: place a large, plastic lawn bag over the top of the tree and pull it down to the trunk before you carry it out. If the tree is too long for one bag, pull up another bag from the bottom.

• Take the tree apart with pruning clippers and put the pieces into a plastic bag. Protect floor area with another bag or cloth to collect fallen needles. Put sandwich bags on your hands when handling the tree trunk to keep off pitch.

> *Santa has an easier time filling stockings when he first separates each child's candy and prizes in resealable bags. That is, after all, how he makes it all the way around the world in one night.*
> *Glenda A. Hardaway, Arlington, TX*

Christmas Storage Solutions

• Use large, plastic garbage bags to hide presents from the kids. Hide the bags in the back of a closet or someplace where it looks as if you're storing out-of-season or outgrown clothes. Or consider storing them in the locked trunk of your car.

• Plastic resealable bags are good for storing delicate Christmas ornaments. Put each one in a separate, self-sealing bag and leave some air in the bag (or blow air in with a straw) before closing it to provide a protective cushion.

• Keep the previous year's card collection in a see-though bag. It is an easy way to have your Christmas card list without actually having to write one out.

> *You know all those parts that come with the"some assembly required" gifts that show up at Christmas time? Self-closing bags are excellent for holding all those parts (little screws, washers, bolts and nuts) while you work on those projects. The added benefit is that you have all of the leftover parts in one spot, so when you find out they are not extras, you know where they are and can complete the required assembly , even if it is June.*
> *Merle Lyons, Scottsdale, AZ*

Halloween Fun

• Use one of the large, plastic leaf bags with the Jack 'O Lantern face as a cape for a devil or witch costume. If the bag has a drawstring, the tie for the cape is already there.

- Or let your child be The Great Pumpkin. Cut leg holes in the bottom of an orange, plastic leaf bag. Pull the bag on and cut armholes where needed. Fill the bag with lightweight stuffing such as crumpled papers. Gather upper edge around neck with masking tape or string. Wear a green hat and green facial make-up.

- Dress your child as Robin Hood with a green, plastic garbage bag belted in the middle, tights and a V-shaped hat made of brown paper. (Companions can come as "Sherwood Forest" by stapling leaves to pajamas and tights.)

At Halloween, I used the self-closing bags to make up Halloween bags for the kids. I put Halloween stickers on the outside of the bags. They looked great.

Kathy J. Chesh, Allentown, PA

- Make an instant Hawaiian grass skirt by cutting narrow strips to within a few inches of one long side of a large, green trash bag.

- Go for the "Layered Monster" look. Pull one large, upside-down, plastic trash bag over your child's shoulders after you have cut an opening for head and slits for hands. Shred the lower edge. Pull another large bag over head and shoulders (after you have cut opening for face); gather up the bag with masking tape around neck and above head; shred bottom edges and add anything else you'd like to the outer bag.

- Make streamers by cutting a plastic garbage bag (black or white or both) into strips (cut almost to the bottom of the bag so streamers stay together) and hang them from the front porch. Fasten them with long pieces of tape so they're low enough to just brush kids' faces as they pass by.

• Make a Goblin Grab Bag from a plastic, orange leaf bag. Fill it with mini party favors that children can reach in and grab.

Clear Plastic or Latex Gloves
While not technically a bag,
plastic gloves can be used for Halloween fun.

Δ Turn gloves inside out, leaving the powdery side to the outside or use the disposable plastic gloves you find in the paint store. Mix your favorite fruit drink (sugar-free liquids freeze better than those with sugar) and pour into the gloves. Add enough drink to fill the gloves loosely, but not so full that the fingers will not move. Fasten the gloves tightly with a twist tie. Place paper towels on a cookie sheet and lay the hands on the paper towels. Freeze. When hands are frozen solid, carefully cut off gloves with scissors. Float "hands" in a punch bowl.

Δ Insert candy corn (to look like a nail) in each finger before filling the gloves with popcorn.

Other Seasonal Ideas

• Use plastic bags to pack and store seasonal items, such as left over holiday greeting cards, Valentines and Halloween decorations, directions and recipes for holiday projects and foods.

• Live in a warm climate, where it doesn't snow often or just want to have un-seasonal fun? When it snows, make snowballs and store them in bags in the freezer, then have a snowball fight on the Fourth of July.

• Dye Easter eggs the easy, no-mess way. Enclose the egg and dye in a resealable bag and shake gently.

• Give kids quart-size, resealable plastic bags for their Easter Egg (*or whatever else you hide*) Hunt. You can decorate the bag with Easter-themed stickers.

> *My children use resealable bags to include candy with their Valentines for school. They put a Valentine and three pieces of candy in each bag and passed them out to everyone in their class. The teacher really liked the idea.*
>
> Katy Emmans, Goshen, IN

Gifts—The Little Things That Count

• Place any small gift item, wrapped in tissue paper, inside a bag for a secure gift wrap. You can add a bow, a card or whatever decorations you like. Let kids decorate bags using permanent markers, glitter or stickers. Or, when it's the season, fill with stocking stuffers or small Chanukah gifts.

• Make decorative gift-wrapping ribbons, using colored plastic bags, by cutting the bags into continuous strips. Then, to be even fancier, you can pull the edges to create a ruffled look.

• Wrap and freeze small batches of plain or colored cookie dough in resealable bags, as gifts for friends. Include a recipe card with baking instructions on the outside.

• Ship a gift of cookies in the mail by putting different flavors and either hard or soft cookies in separate bags, so taste and texture won't be affected.

A Final, Charitable, Thought

Use resealable bags to make up and hold personal toiletries kits to donate to a homeless shelter or prison. You can use sample sizes collected from trips, items purchased on sale or given as a donation.

Chapter Four

ASSORTED OTHER SACKS

While paper and plastic bags have become staples of our everyday life, there are still other carrying containers that have their special place. While some of these fall into the disposable category, others—like canvas bags—don't. There is much to be said in favor of using our own carry-alls when shopping, in that it truly is a help to the environment. Some grocery stores give customers a credit of a few cents for every reusable bag they bring with them. It is a simple way anyone can start to "make a difference." That's something to think about.

NET PRODUCE BAGS

These are the sturdy bags that can hold weighty items such as onions or potatoes, while allowing air to circulate around the contents. While disposable, they, too, can have a second life. A lighter weight net is also used in some Christmas "stocking" packages. These bags, too, can be reused with many of the suggestions listed below. Mesh, still another material used for bags, comes in a large, open weave as well as a small weave and is usually made of nylon.

Outside/Garden

• Store bulbs in mesh bags hung in the garage or a dry basement so the air can circulate around them.

• Dry large-petaled flowers, to be used later for homemade potpourri, in a mesh bag.

• For fast cleanups outside, hang a bar of soap in a mesh bag on an outside faucet. To wash your hands, just rub them on the mesh bag and they will soap up. Rinse your hands using the water faucet.

• Carry toys to the beach in a mesh bag. When it's time to leave, wash off the toys, in the bag, allow to drain and take them home minus the sand.

• Make your own suet ball. Pack suet into a mesh bag and hang it from a sturdy branch for the birds to enjoy. It is better to use as a winter or cool-weather food. In hot weather, it attracts bees.

In the Kitchen

• Use a mesh bag to hold small items that will go through your dishwasher.

• Scrub vegetables, such as carrots or potatoes, with pieces cut from a mesh bag.

• Put tomatoes you plan to freeze or can in a mesh bag and submerge in a pot of boiling water for one minute, then peel their skins off easily.

• Store potatoes and onions in vented mesh bags, instead of plastic, and hang or store them in a cool, dry place. Because air can circulate around the items and the bag doesn't retain dampness, they will keep longer.

• Tie a bit of mesh filled with leftover bits of soap around a sponge or dishcloth as an "automatic" soap dispenser.

For Household Odds 'n Ends

• Place a rolled-up mesh bag in the bottom of a vase to help hold long-stem flowers in place.

• Make a basketball hoop out of a mesh bag. Cut the ends off and thread a straightened hanger through the top, forming a circle. Hang it over a door, using the hook part of the hanger.

• Or create a butterfly net or fishing net for kids. Again, make a hoop, using either a hanger or stiff wire, then secure the ends of the wire into a handle.

- Hang a heavy net bag from the tub faucet or showerhead to hold bathtub toys and allow them to drip dry.

- Keep two or more balls of yarn or embroidery thread clean and untangled throughout a project. Place them in a mesh bag and thread the ends through holes on opposite sides of the bag.

NYLON NET AND MESH BAGS

Nylon netting and nylon mesh, a softer, finer fabric, are both used for recyclable bags that hold various foods or other products. Mesh bags for specific purposes, such as laundering delicate items, are sold in department stores or specialty shops and can be used indefinitely.

- Cut nylon net bags into strips and tie together in a pom-pom, or gather them and bind them around the center with a string or rubber band—you'll have a pot scrubber that won't scratch your cookware. The original 'Heloise' made much of this idea, suggesting nylon netting bought by the yard as fabric.

- Make a scrubbing pad by folding the pieces of a net bag into a square of the size desired and sewing on all four sides.

- Use a piece cut from a net bag to hold in place baseball hats or visors which you wash on the top shelf of the dishwasher. Secure items in place by looping the mesh on the rack separators.

Purchased Mesh Bags
- Tuck soap slivers into a mesh bag to use at the kitchen sink or in the bathtub as you would a bar of soap.

- Make your own air freshener. Bake apple and orange peels on a cookie sheet at 200°F for four or five hours, or until thoroughly dried. Mix the dried peels with whole cloves, nutmeg and bits of cinnamon sticks, and put the mixture into a small mesh bag you suspend on a hanger in a closet.

- Keep fabric belts and scarves from tangling with other washables by tucking them into the mesh bag you use for lingerie in the washer.

- Hang a net bag from the inside of your locker at the health club to hold your toiletries. It makes it easy to transport everything to the shower and it allows all to air dry once back in your locker.

- Wash a child's favorite stuffed toy safely in a mesh bag.

- Line a wastebasket with a nylon mesh bag and use it as a laundry hamper for socks. When it's full, zip it up and throw it in the washer and dryer. Keep an extra bag in the bottom, so there's always one on hand.

- Use several mesh bags to hold pickles you wash in your washing machine in preparation for canning. The bags will protect them while still allowing them to get clean.

CANVAS BAGS

Canvas bags are usually not free. They are great for hauling "stuff" of every definition. They come in all sizes, can be bought with your favorite designs, and many also come with advertisements that are status symbols. Known to many as "schlep" bags, they last a long time. They are machine washable, but should be air dried.

The really large ones, such as those that Lands' End and L.L. Bean sell, are called "rigger bags"—a nautical connotation, as boating people seem to use them.

They're also great for travel in a car or plane. As carry-ons, they hold up better than plastic, which, when overstuffed, has been known to break, usually at an inopportune moment.

Many are not flat-bottomed, which makes a difference in their usefulness. Because they do dry out, they make good carry-alls for damp items or at the beach or poolside.

• Use smaller canvas totes in your closet, over a hanger, to separate and store such accessories as belts and scarves.

• Assign a canvas bag for each family member to hold winter mittens, hats and scarves in the coat closet.

• Bring a canvas bag or two, especially at warehouse clubs that offer little in the way of carryout containers.

• Designate one to hold all laundry products you need when visiting the laundromat.

• Or for cleaning supplies (rags, feather duster, and such) that you need as you move from room to room when you clean.

• Hang a canvas bag from a nail on the wall of your garage to store athletic equipment. Use a different bag for each sport category.

• Pack an extra one in a suitcase to use on trips for all those "must have" items you accumulate while traveling that you don't think will add up to much until you try and fit them all in the suitcase.

• Use all available canvas bags when moving and you'll have fewer boxes to dispose of.

• Make canvas-like hanging pouches by cutting out pockets from old demin pants or jackets.

HANDBAGS

How can one not discuss the most useful bag of all—at least for women—the handbag? Their recycle value is limited, but their importance in our lives goes beyond utilitarian. They are fashion statements, reflect our lifestyles and even become a source of security. (If you've ever had your handbag stolen, you know how violated you feel.) Our purses are the closest thing to us, except for family, friends and pets. If you have occasion to visit a dining room in a nursing home, I think you will see most women there still carrying their handbags—and it's not to pay for the meal. So, a handbag is not just a bag.

In Conclusion

I suspect you really didn't think there were this many great uses for bags. I certainly didn't! And though I can't promise you I'll be able to include additional ones in future editions, I would still love to hear from you, if you know of a terrific use for a bag—paper, plastic or otherwise. Send it to me (*on a postcard, please*) to the following address:

Vicki Lansky
c/o Book Peddlers
15245 Minnetonka Blvd
Minnetonka, MN 55345

or e-mail me at:
DearVicki@aol.com

Index